Behavior Modification: Basic Principles

Managing Behavior Series

Behavior Modification: Basic Principles
Behavior Modification: The Measurement of Behavior

Behavior Modification: Basic Principles

SECOND EDITION

Saul Axelrod
R. Vance Hall

An International Publisher

8700 Shoal Creek Boulevard
Austin, Texas 78757-6897
800/897-3202 Fax 800/397-7633
Order online at http://www.proedinc.com

© 1999, 1975, 1971 by PRO-ED, Inc.
8700 Shoal Creek Boulevard
Austin, Texas 78757-6897
800/897-3202 Fax 800/397-7633
Order online at http://www.proedinc.com

All rights reserved. No part of the material protected by this copyright notice may be reproduced or used in any form or by any means, electronic or mechanical, including photocopying, recording, or by any information storage and retrieval system, without the prior written permission of the copyright owner.

Library of Congress Cataloging-in-Publication Data

Axelrod, Saul.
    Behavior modification : basic principles / Saul Axelrod, R. Vance Hall. —2nd ed.
      p. cm.
    Rev. ed. of part 2 of three parts of the original ed. of Behavior management series published in 1969.
    ISBN 0-89079-804-4 (alk. paper)
    1. Behavior modification.   I. Hall, R. Vance (Robert Vance), 1928–
II. Title
BF637.B4 A94   1999
                                                  98-30834
                                                     CIP

This book is designed in Palatino and Frutiger.

Production Director: Alan Grimes
Production Coordinator: Dolly Fisk Jackson
Managing Editor: Chris Olson
Art Director: Thomas Barkley
Designer: Jason Crosier
Print Buyer: Alicia Woods
Preproduction Coordinator: Chris Anne Worsham
Staff Copyeditor: Martin Wilson
Publishing Assistant: John Means Cooper

Printed in the United States of America

1 2 3 4 5 6 7 8 9 10   03 02 01 00 99

153.85
Ax 22b

Contents

Preface ▪ ix

Introduction ▪ 1

Operant Behavior ▪ 1

The Causes of Respondent and Operant Behavior ▪ 1

Respondent Conditioning ▪ 1

Operant Conditioning ▪ 2

Reinforcement ▪ 2
    Immediacy of Reinforcement ▪ 3
    Reinforcement Must Be Contingent ▪ 3
    Varying the Reinforcers ▪ 4

Basic Principles Quiz 1 ▪ 4

Establishing Reinforcers ▪ 7
    Primary Reinforcers ▪ 7
    Secondary Reinforcers ▪ 7
    Individualizing Reinforcement ▪ 8
    Generalized Reinforcers ▪ 8
    Deprivation and Satiation ▪ 9

Basic Principles Quiz 2 ▪ 9

Reinforcement Operations ▪ 10
    Positive Reinforcement ▪ 10
    Negative Reinforcement ▪ 11

Basic Principles Quiz 3 ▪ 12

Types of Positive Reinforcers ▪ 13
    Tangible Reinforcers ▪ 13
    Activity Reinforcers ▪ 13
    Social Reinforcement ▪ 14
    Token Reinforcers ▪ 16

Basic Principles Quiz 4 ▪ 18

Selecting Appropriate Reinforcers ▪ 20

Potential Reinforcers for Ages 0–4 at Home ▪ 21

Potential Reinforcers for Ages 5–11 at Home ▪ 22

Potential Reinforcers for Ages 12–18 at Home ▪ 23

Potential Reinforcers for Elementary School Pupils ▪ 24

Potential Reinforcers for Secondary School Pupils ▪ 25

Potential Reinforcers on the Job ▪ 25

Potential Reinforcers for Spouses/Significant Others ▪ 26

Basic Principles Quiz 5 ▪ 28

Applying Reinforcement ▪ 30
    Contingency Contracting ▪ 30

Opportunities To Respond and Three-Term Contingencies ▪ 31

Teaching New Behaviors Through Shaping ▪ 33

Schedules of Reinforcement ▪ 35

Intermittent Schedules of Reinforcement ▪ 35
    Ratio Schedules ▪ 35
    Interval Schedules ▪ 37

Feedback ▪ 39

Basic Principles Quiz 6 ▪ 39

Procedures for Decreasing Behavior ▪ 41
    Decreasing Behavior Through Extinction ▪ 42
    Decreasing Behavior Through Reinforcement ▪ 45
    Decreasing Behavior Through Punishment ▪ 45
    Some Effective Punishment Procedures ▪ 47

Basic Principles Quiz 7 ▪ 50

Antecedents of Behavior ▪ 53
    Stimulus Control ▪ 54

Generalization and Discrimination ▪ 54

Instructional Control ▪ 56

Modeling and Imitation ▪ 56

Prompting and Fading ▪ 57
    Verbal Prompts ▪ 58
    Gestural Prompts ▪ 58
    Physical Prompts ▪ 58
    Prompts that Remain ▪ 59

Behavioral Chains ▪ 60

Basic Principles Quiz 8 ▪ 62

Basic Principles Final Examination ▪ 66

Answers to Basic Principles Quizzes ▪ 73
    Quiz 1 ▪ 73
    Quiz 2 ▪ 74
    Quiz 3 ▪ 74
    Quiz 4 ▪ 74
    Quiz 5 ▪ 75
    Quiz 6 ▪ 75
    Quiz 7 ▪ 76
    Quiz 8 ▪ 76

Answers to Basic Principles Final Examination ▪ 78

References and Further Reading ▪ 81

About the Authors ▪ 83

Preface

The original Managing Behavior series was published in 1969. At that time few texts were available to introduce students to what was then called behavior modification. The original series contained three parts: *The Measurement of Behavior, Basic Principles,* and *Applications in School and Home.* Since that first edition some thirty years ago, the series has been revised and *Applications in School and Home* has been discontinued. This book provided examples of behavior analysis studies carried out by parents and teachers. Today many such studies are available in the literature, something not true when the original edition was published.

Since their first publication, more than 300,000 copies each of *Observation and Measurement of Behavior* and *Basic Principles* have been sold; they have been translated into Spanish, Portuguese, Hebrew, Dutch, and French. Thousands of students and practitioners have received their first introduction to behavior analysis through these booklets. The books are still being widely used because the information is presented in a simple, straightforward, and easy-to-understand manner.

The approach in the first of this two-part series, *The Measurement of Behavior,* is to teach the reader to observe and measure behaviors that they wish to change as simply as possible. The second part, *Basic Principles,* presents the basic principles of behavior emphasizing the use of consequences naturally available in the home, business, or school environment to modify those behaviors. This approach differs from some behavioral models that stress the use of complex graphing of data, extrinsic reinforcers, and complex reinforcer systems and equipment.

This revised edition of *Behavior Modification: Basic Principles* has been expanded to provide clearer and more comprehensive examples for the reader. In addition, the revision includes sections on feedback and three-term contingencies.

The authors are indebted to the many students, teachers, parents, and others who helped develop these materials, and to the many people who have shared with us their experiences in the successful application of behavior management techniques in home, school, work, and community environments. We are further indebted to Steve Mathews of PRO-ED, who provided assistance and encouragement on this revision.

Saul Axelrod
R. Vance Hall

Introduction

Behavior refers to anything a person does. Driving to work, eating a sandwich, and blinking one's eyes are all examples of behavior. B. F. Skinner, the modern founder of behavior analysis, noted that there are two types of behavior. The first is called *respondent behavior* and refers to reflexive or involuntary behavior. Examples include perspiring in the presence of heat and salivating in the presence of food. Respondent behaviors are *elicited*, meaning automatic, since heat automatically causes perspiration and food automatically causes salivation. The second type of behavior is *operant behavior* and will be the focus of this text.

Operant Behavior

Operant behaviors are voluntary behaviors. Examples include a father carrying his daughter on his shoulders, a student raising his or her hand in class, and a person working on a computer. Operant behavior was so named because it operates on, or affects, the environment. The environment, in turn, operates on or affects behavior in some manner. Operant behaviors are said to be *emitted*, unlike respondent behaviors which are elicited.

The Causes of Respondent and Operant Behavior

The term *stimulus* refers to any change in the environment. Some stimuli come before a behavior, and some come after a behavior. Respondent behaviors are controlled by stimuli that precede the behavior. Thus, heat precedes perspiration and food precedes salivation. The stimuli that elicit respondent behaviors are known as *unconditioned stimuli*. Operant behaviors, on the other hand, are controlled by stimuli that follow the behavior. Thus, praise or criticism following a behavior will likely change the rate of the behavior. These stimuli are called *consequent stimuli*, or more simply, *consequences*.

Respondent Conditioning

It is possible for a neutral stimulus to acquire the ability to elicit a respondent behavior. The process, first discovered by Russian psychologist Ivan Pavlov in his work with dogs, is known as *respondent* or *classical conditioning*. Pavlov noted that a bell was originally neutral in its ability to produce salivation from a dog (i.e., the bell alone did not elicit salivation). Yet, when the bell was repeatedly presented shortly before food was introduced, the dog salivated simply from the presentation of the bell. Thus, the bell acquired the capacity to elicit salivation and was called a *conditioned stimulus*. Of course, when Pavlov presented only the bell and not the food, the bell eventually lost its ability to elicit salivation, a process identified as *respondent extinction*.

Emotional behavior is respondent behavior. When emotional behavior occurs in the classroom, in the home, or on the job, it can interfere with learning and performance. Stimuli associated with powerful punishers often elicit strong emotional responses. For example, if a teacher uses criticism, ridicule, or physical punishment, it is likely that emotional responses will be elicited. In addition, because of respondent conditioning, the subject, the classroom, and the teacher, all of which are frequently paired with these stimuli, may come to elicit emotional responses. Thus, for these children, even coming into the presence of the teacher or being told that it is time for the reading period may result in emotional behavior that will interfere with learning. Sometimes school-phobic children become physically ill on entering the school building. To prevent this or to overcome the situation once it has occurred, educators need to make certain that criticism and other forms of punishment are not paired with a school setting for a considerable period in order to allow for respondent extinction. Better yet, praise for appropriate behavior can replace criticism for inappropriate behavior.

Operant Conditioning

Operant conditioning refers to the process by which the consequences of behavior change the future rate of the behavior. If the consequences are pleasant, the behavior will occur more frequently in the future. If the consequences are unpleasant, the behavior will occur less frequently in the future. For example, if a student volunteers an answer in class and receives a teacher's compliment, it is likely that the child will answer more questions in the future. On the other hand, if an employee volunteers for extra work, but is ridiculed by his boss for his performance, he is unlikely to volunteer in the future.

Reinforcement

Reinforcement is the process by which the consequences of a behavior increase the future rate of that behavior. In other words, a person performs a behavior and experiences a consequence. If the behavior occurs more frequently in the future than it did in the past, reinforcement is said to have occurred. For example, if a mother makes a deal with her teenage son that she will pay him to mow the lawn, and he does so more frequently in the future, the mother has used a reinforcement procedure.

Often a person cannot tell whether something is a reinforcer until she tries it out. First, she would note how often the behavior occurred under normal, or *baseline,* conditions. Then she would try out the potential reinforcement procedure. Only if the behavior increases in rate could she say she had used a reinforcement procedure.

Immediacy of Reinforcement

It is not uncommon to hear someone say, "Oh, I tried reinforcement and that stuff doesn't work." Frequently, the reason the procedure doesn't work is because the person did not provide reinforcement immediately after the behavior. *Reinforcement must immediately follow the desired behavior in order to have its maximum effect.* It is important to deliver a reinforcer immediately after a behavior occurs because that behavior will then become most closely associated with the reinforcer. If reinforcement is delayed, the consequences might become associated with a different behavior. Thus, teachers who move around the classroom and compliment correct answers are more effective than teachers who stay in one place. Giving out bonuses for outstanding performance should be done monthly or quarterly, rather than annually. Parents who use toys as reinforcers for weekly improvement in school should have the toys available at the end of the week, rather than purchasing them on the weekend.

▶ **Assignment:** Suggest how the following people might more immediately reinforce behavior than is commonly the case: a parent, a teacher, a professor, an employer, yourself.

Reinforcement Must Be Contingent

An increase in pay will not necessarily make employees more productive. Similarly, giving students extra free time will not automatically get them to work harder. If reinforcement is such a good procedure, why won't these reinforcers always work? What is missing is that the bonuses are not contingent on the behavior. *Reinforcement must be contingent on the desired behavior in order to increase the future likelihood of the behavior.*

A contingent relationship is an *if–then* relationship. *If* the desired behavior occurs, *then* the reinforcer will be delivered. Thus, increases in pay must be contingent on increased employee productivity, and extra free time must be contingent on appropriate student behavior.

▶ **Assignment:** A mother says to her daughter, "As soon as you are done calling your friends, I want you to set the table and do your homework." What is wrong with this picture? What should the mother be saying?

Varying the Reinforcers

If someone uses the same reinforcer over and over again, the reinforcer may lose its value. *When using reinforcement procedures, it is better to use a variety of reinforcers.* For example, when delivering compliments, a person can use expressions such as "Very good," "Wonderful," "Nicely done," and "I am really impressed." Parents can treat their children to a movie on one occasion and a trip to a sporting event on another. When employers give their staff a financial bonus, a variety of reinforcers are inherent, since money can be used to purchase a multitude of items.

A person's receptivity to a reinforcer is different at different times. Thus, a person who enters a health club might rush to an open treadmill. Thirty minutes later, the treadmill is of no appeal. A child who has unlimited access to television will not work for the opportunity to watch television. Thus, limiting the ordinary availability of a potential reinforcer is an important factor in creating its appeal.

Basic Principles Quiz 1

1. Define *stimulus*.

2. In respondent behavior, does a stimulus *precede* or *follow* a response?

3. Discuss the differences between respondent and operant behaviors.

4. Respondent conditioning occurs when we repeatedly pair a neutral stimulus with an unconditioned stimulus until the neutral stimulus

(continues)

5. Respondent extinction occurs when the conditioned stimulus is presented repeatedly

_____
_____.

6. If school has been repeatedly paired with stimuli that elicit strong emotional responses, what needs to be done?

_____
_____
_____
_____
_____

7. Define *operant conditioning.*

_____
_____
_____
_____

Give an example of operant conditioning.

_____
_____
_____
_____
_____
_____

(*continues*)

8. Define *reinforcement*.

9. To maximize the effectiveness of a reinforcement procedure, the following three conditions must be met:

10. Give everyday examples of how reinforcement is used in the following environments:

    Home:

    School:

(continues)

Work:

_____

_____

_____

Establishing Reinforcers

There is no such thing as a universal reinforcer. Some consequences will be reinforcing to some people, but not to others. One student or employee might find a compliment reinforcing, whereas another might find it embarrassing or annoying. Therefore, it is important to learn how to select reinforcers and to understand how certain events become reinforcers.

Primary Reinforcers

Consequences that serve a biological need are known as *primary* or *unconditioned reinforcers.* Common primary reinforcers include food when a person is hungry, drink when a person is thirsty, sleep when a person is tired, and warmth when a person is cold. Primary reinforcers may be dependent on a state of biological deprivation, but their ability to alter behavior is genetic and is therefore not learned. *A primary reinforcer does not depend on previous conditioning for its reinforcing power.*

Secondary Reinforcers

Food, drink, warmth, and sexual stimulation are important reinforcers, but make up a small part of the consequent stimuli that reinforce behavior. In general, it is not desirable to use only primary reinforcers to change behavior. Parents, teachers, and employers do not want people to work only for food, for example, as a reinforcer. It is more desirable that people work for consequences such as praise, attention, and merit pay. Such reinforcers are more likely to be available in the natural environment and are more socially acceptable than primary reinforcers. Thus, a second kind of reinforcer is a *secondary* or *conditioned reinforcer.* These are events that have *acquired* their reinforcing power.

How do things such as praise and money, which originally have no meaning to a person, become secondary reinforcers? This is achieved through the process of *pairing* the event with another reinforcer. For example, if a mother continually praises her son while she is nursing him, the words of praise become associated with food and then become secondary reinforcers.

Most reinforcers available to parents, teachers, and employers are of the secondary type. Thus, it is possible to reinforce behavior with a kind word, a complimentary note, or a certificate of recognition. It is important to note that if the secondary reinforcer is no longer associated with another reinforcer, it may lose its ability to reinforce behavior. For example, if an employee keeps winning the Employee of the Month award, but never gets a raise in pay, she might leave her present employment for another job.

> ▶ **Problem:** Suppose you are the teacher or a parent of a student who is not motivated by grades. How could you make grades into conditioned reinforcers?

Individualizing Reinforcement

Events that are reinforcing to one person may not be reinforcing to another person. (Remember the expression, "That's why they make vanilla and chocolate.") Still, some events are reinforcing to many people. Most young people find free time reinforcing, and most adults find money to be a powerful reinforcer.

In cases where the typical conditioned reinforcers are not effective, it may be necessary to turn to primary reinforcers or conditioned reinforcers not commonly used in that situation. These reinforcers can then be paired with more common reinforcers, such as praise, attention, privileges, smiles, and good grades, until the latter become reinforcing. Thus, sometimes it is necessary to pair verbal praise and attention with hugs, pats on the head, or even food for a child who does not initially respond to adult attention. After a time, the conditioned reinforcers will begin to take hold and physical contact and food can be reduced.

This process occurs naturally in our society with most children. When a child is young, parents and teachers use hugs, pats on the head, and other overt expressions as reinforcers. As the child becomes older, his teachers, parents, and employers are more likely to use praise, smiles, and forms of attention other than physical contact.

Generalized Reinforcers

A reinforcer that has been associated with many other reinforcers is known as a *generalized conditioned reinforcer,* or more simply as a *generalized reinforcer.* Praise, for example, is a generalized reinforcer for most people, since it has been paired with approval, extra dessert, and raises in pay. Still, no event is a conditioned reinforcer for all people. Thus, some people will reject praise, and some people have no use for paper money.

▶ **Question:** Why is money a powerful generalized reinforcer for most people?

Deprivation and Satiation

For a reinforcer to be effective, it is necessary that there be a state of deprivation for that reinforcer. One reason that generalized reinforcers work so well is that they are not affected by any single state of deprivation or satiation. For example, money is still reinforcing to a person who has just seen a movie, because money can then be used to purchase a snack.

Deprivation relates to how long it has been since reinforcement was last available. For example, a snack of milk and cookies is much more likely to be reinforcing at 4:00 p.m. than right after lunch.

Satiation occurs when too much of a given reinforcer is delivered at one time. (A teacher who says "very good" to her pupils over and over may make that form of praise ineffective.) In fact, some reinforcers (including food) may become unappealing if presented in large enough quantities in a short period of time. It is important to vary the type of reinforcer used and to use generalized reinforcers which do not depend on a single deprivation state in most situations. It should be noted, however, that very few teachers, parents, or employers provide too much reinforcement. Most people err on the side of providing too little reinforcement for appropriate behavior.

Basic Principles Quiz 2

1. Distinguish between a primary and a secondary reinforcer.

   _____

   _____

2. Give three examples of primary reinforcers and three examples of secondary reinforcers not mentioned in this book.

   _____

   _____

   _____

   _____

   _____

(continues)

3. How can a smiley face be established as a generalized reinforcer?

4. Describe a person in your environment who has a behavior in need of modification. Describe in detail the potential steps you might go through to determine a reinforcer for the person's behavior.

Reinforcement Operations

There are two types of reinforcement operations: *positive* and *negative*. Both types have the effect of increasing the probability of the behavior that precedes the reinforcer. Negative reinforcement should not be confused with punishment, which is described later in the text.

Positive Reinforcement

In a positive reinforcement operation, a person performs a behavior and then something that person likes is *presented*. If the future rate of that behavior increases, positive reinforcement has occurred. Examples of this procedure are endless: a baby smiling at his parents when he is picked up; a teacher praising his class for working quietly during study period; a child thanking a parent for buying candy at the store; and a father who gives an extra 50 cents in allowance when his son helps around the house. The technique of adding something good contingent on desired behavior has the distinct advantage of causing the person and the situation associated with that reinforcer to become positive reinforcers. In other words, employers, parents, teachers, and children who have learned to add good things become well-liked and effective reinforcing agents. The procedure they use, whether they know it or not, is positive reinforcement. The only way to receive such reinforcement is to come in contact with the person who uses it.

Positive reinforcement is the heart and soul of behaviorism. Its introduction into psychology and education gave people an alternative to the age-old practice of punishing undesirable behavior. In a successful positive reinforcement procedure, only winners exist. People who receive positive reinforcement glow with pride and excitement. Parents, teachers, and employers feel good about themselves when they reinforce behavior and see favorable results.

Negative Reinforcement

When a positive reinforcement procedure is used, a person performs a behavior and receives something he likes. This causes the person to perform the behavior more frequently in the future. A second type of reinforcement is negative reinforcement. With this operation a person performs a behavior to avoid or escape something he dislikes. This type of reinforcement also has the effect of increasing the future rate of the behavior. Although negative reinforcement is a less obvious procedure than positive reinforcement, its occurrence is common. When a mother tells her daughter that she doesn't have to help with the dishes if she finishes her peas, and the child quickly consumes her peas, negative reinforcement has occurred. Other examples of negative reinforcement occur when a teacher tells students that they will not have homework if they finish their reading assignment on time; when a professor allows students to skip the final examination if their semester average exceeds 90%; and when a supervisor allows her employees to have a day off if all work is done early. If all of these cases produce the desired increase in behavior, they qualify as negative reinforcement. Doing the dishes, doing homework, taking the final examination, and being at work were the negative reinforcers in the above situations.

Negative reinforcement can produce desirable or undesirable outcomes. A desirable outcome was achieved in a case cited above when students worked hard to complete their assignment and avoided having to do homework. An undesirable example of negative reinforcement occurs when an employee argues with his supervisor every time she gives him a difficult assignment. If the supervisor withdraws the assignment, she has negatively reinforced arguing and should expect arguing to occur in similar situations in the future.

Although positive and negative reinforcement operations both result in increases in behavior, it is usually better to use positive reinforcement whenever possible. That is, it is better to have people work to achieve things they like rather than have them work to avoid or escape things they dislike. One problem with negative reinforcement operations is that people may sometimes avoid the environment in which the negative reinforcers occur. For example, a father might nag his daughter until she finishes her homework and cleans her room. One way the daughter can avoid the nagging is to finish her homework and clean her room, thus qualifying as negative reinforcement. On the other hand, the daughter can avoid the nagging simply by finding an excuse to stay away from the house.

Sometimes it is difficult to distinguish between positive and negative reinforcement. When a person turns on a light, for example, is she adding light (positive reinforcement) or removing darkness (negative reinforcement)? The answer is unclear and unimportant. What is important is that people use procedures to increase behavior and that, when possible, they program for the addition of pleasant consequences, rather than the removal of unpleasant consequences.

Basic Principles Quiz 3

Mike appeared to be an excellent father to his new daughter, Mindy. He gave her a lot of attention and affection. Nevertheless, Mindy typically cried when she saw her father. She continued crying until he picked her up, which he invariably did.

   1. What procedure is Mindy applying to her father's behavior?

   _____

   _____

   2. What procedure is Mike applying to Mindy's behavior?

   _____

   _____

   3. How are positive reinforcement and negative reinforcement similar?

   _____

   _____

(*continues*)

4. How are they different?

_____

_____

_____

_____

Types of Positive Reinforcers

There are four different classifications of positive reinforcers: tangible, social, activity, and token.

Tangible reinforcers: material items such as food, toys, magazines, comic books, coloring books, clothes, and appliances

Activity reinforcers: privileges such as having free time, having extra computer time, receiving a day off from work, attending a movie, listening to a CD, and being classroom messenger

Social reinforcers: Employee of the Month, letters of congratulation, handshakes, pats on the back, attention, praise, and notes home from teachers

Token reinforcers: any symbols such as a check mark, smiley face, or gift certificate that can be exchanged for something of value

Tangible Reinforcers

Consumable and other types of tangible reinforcers, such as candy, trinkets, and toys, can be powerful motivators for human behavior. Also, in working with some populations, such as people with severe impairments, a reinforcer such as food might be the only effective one available. However, in most cases one should look for alternatives, because tangible reinforcers are often expensive, and because many people find it socially unacceptable to use these reinforcers, such as candy reinforcers for high school students and portable radios for adult employees. The alternatives described below are both powerful and socially acceptable.

Activity Reinforcers

Favorite activities undoubtedly constitute a powerful type of reinforcer. Also, many appealing activity reinforcers are free or inexpensive. Effective activity reinforcers in the schools include free time, helping the secretary or custodian, lining up first, being a messenger, and handing out papers. Activity reinforcers in the home include being allowed to stay up late, going out for a pizza or to a movie, and having a friend sleep over. Activity reinforcers in the workplace include parking in a preferred spot, receiving favored job assignments, using preferred restrooms, and having lunch with and paid for by the boss.

We highly recommend the use of activity reinforcers. However, some problems might be encountered with their use. First, some activities such as free time in a school might result in disorderly play and might be disruptive to other classes. Also, it is not always possible to provide activity reinforcers in a timely manner, thus resulting in a delay of reinforcement. Finally, some activity reinforcers such as attending a sports event on a certain date must be provided on an all-or-none basis, limiting its flexible application.

Social Reinforcement

No form of reinforcement is less expensive and easier to deliver than social reinforcement. Examples of social reinforcers include compliments, handshakes, smiles, words of appreciation, letters of commendation, honor rolls, and award certificates. The most common form of social reinforcement is praise. Praise can be delivered immediately after a behavior occurs, costs nothing, is not disruptive to the surrounding environment, and requires no preparation for its delivery. Examples of praise include such comments as, "Thanks for getting the job done so quickly," "You are really paying attention today," and "I really like the way you helped him with his geometry lesson." The following is a list of guidelines on the use of praise:

1. Make praise contingent on appropriate behavior. If it is used indiscriminately it will reinforce both inappropriate and appropriate behaviors.

2. Praise should sound sincere. Sincerity can be achieved by making eye contact with the person and varying the compliments. Instead of saying "Very good!" over and over, try saying "Fantastic!," "Cool!," "That's decent," or other terms in vogue at the moment. Also, vary the expression and inflection in your voice—show varying amounts of enthusiasm.

3. When listening, learn to smile, give eye contact, and ask questions about what the other person says. Few things are more reinforcing. On the other hand, persons who merely wait to jump in and say what they want to say are very offensive.

4. Pair social reinforcement with other reinforcers by lending a helping hand or giving other reinforcers with a smile and a word of praise.

5. Become skilled at private, indirect, and public praise. You can provide private praise with a handshake, a quiet word, a written note, or a drawing of a happy face. From a distance, private praise is possible through a smile, a

gesture, a silently mouthed word, a nod of the head, or a wink. People who become skilled at emitting such behaviors are people we tend to like and we are more likely to respond to them in the same way.

6. Another important skill is the use of social reinforcement in conjunction with whatever other reinforcers are used. If we frequently praise or show approval as we provide other reinforcers, a number of positive results are likely to occur:

a. The person with whom we are working will be more likely to find the praise and positive attention of others reinforcing. That is sometimes the only reinforcer available.

b. Our presence may become reinforcing to the person and our attention and interest will be more effective in other situations.

c. Since others learn a great deal through imitation, the persons with whom we come in contact will much more likely learn to reinforce others with positive attention. This is one of the most important skills anyone can learn.

7. We should learn to be specific in our praise. Research has shown that specific praise is usually more effective than general praise. Thus, a teacher will be a more effective reinforcing agent if she tells Herb, "That's such good work! You worked five out of six problems correctly," than if she says, "It looks like you're working better, Herb. I'm proud of you." Being specific helps clarify what behavior resulted in the praise. In this case, correct answers rather than sitting quietly and not disturbing neighbors produced praise. In the same way, the boss's statement, "Sally, I really appreciate how you stayed late and typed up that report without errors. It helped me make that sale," will likely be more effective than, "Sally, you're a good secretary. Thanks for all you do."

In spite of almost universal agreement that people should use praise regularly, it is a seldom used procedure. Parents might go days without complimenting their well-behaved children. Teachers might use praise once an hour, when they could be using it once a minute. Employers might go years without putting a complimentary note in an employee's mailbox. If social reinforcement is such a good procedure, why do so few people use it? One possibility is that some people feel insincere when praising others. This problem is likely to be alleviated as one continually uses praise and when such praise encounters a pleasant reaction from the recipient. A more likely problem is that appropriate behavior does not call attention to itself. In other words, it is a "squeaky wheel" problem. There are at least two ways to overcome this difficulty. One is to have a timer go off at different intervals. At those times, a teacher or a factory supervisor could check to see who is working appropriately and praise those who are. A second way is to keep track of the number of times one uses praise each day and to try to increase the daily total. To keep a record, a person could use a wrist counter or another type of counter.

▶ **Assignment:**

1. For two or three days next week, keep track of the rate at which you deliver social praise to an individual or group. Then try to increase the rate by 3, 5, or even 10 or more times. Report on the results.
2. Try using some reinforcers that are novel to you.
3. Practice using specific praise, public praise, and praise from a distance.

Token Reinforcers

A generalized reinforcer that is useful in a variety of environments is the token reinforcer. A token can be a symbol such as a check mark or a smiley face, or it can be a tangible item such as a trading stamp, a poker chip, a ticket, or a star. In most cases, awarding a token alone will not affect behavior. Tokens, however, can be quite powerful when they are exchangeable for a variety of other items or activities, known as *back-up reinforcers.* Tokens are similar to money in that they can be exchanged for tickets to shows, gift certificates, field trips, and special privileges. Parents use a token reinforcement procedure when they put stars on a calendar for appropriate behavior and allow their children to exchange them for a favored item. Teachers use token systems when they rate a student's behavior on a scale of 1 to 10 four times each day and then allow her to exchange the points for extra computer time. Companies use token systems when they award salespeople free trips for successfully completing a specified number of sales.

Token reinforcement systems are effective for a variety of reasons:

1. The awarding of tokens in a classroom does not disrupt the environment, as does the immediate awarding of activity reinforcers.
2. Since tokens are associated with many back-up reinforcers, they do not depend on any one condition of deprivation (as might be the case with a single food reinforcer).
3. Tokens can be delivered immediately after an appropriate behavior occurs. Other reinforcers cannot be.
4. Since tokens are tangible and can be seen by the recipient, they provide continuous feedback to the learner.

5. Tokens can be broken into small segments and, therefore, allow for graded reinforcement. For example, 25 tokens can be exchanged for one day without having to do household chores, whereas 50 tokens can be exchanged for two days.

6. Tokens can be exchanged for unusual or expensive reinforcers. A child, for example, could work several weeks for a trip to a theme park.

7. Tokens help teachers, parents, and employers set clear goals.

8. There is no maximum number of tokens a person can earn.

9. Token systems help people learn to delay gratification (while still providing immediate feedback).

10. Token systems can be used with one individual, several individuals, or an entire group.

11. Token systems are typically more powerful than other reinforcement systems.

In order to set up a token reinforcement system, certain elements must be in place. First, the desired behaviors need to be specified. Second, the back-up reinforcers must be clear. Third, a clear relationship must exist between the desired behaviors, the tokens, and the back-up reinforcers. For example, getting 20 problems correct can be worth five tokens, which are exchangeable for a short break; or receiving the Employee of the Month award three times can be exchanged for an extra week of vacation. Finally, the time at which the back-up reinforcers may be purchased must be clear.

Sometimes it is necessary to use tokens and tangible reinforcers to condition naturally available reinforcers. Children, who have never responded to natural reinforcers such as adult approval or pride in a job well done, will work hard for tokens that allow them to have things they want or to do things they want to do. After they come into contact with adult approval and have been praised for a job well done as they receive tokens, the tokens can usually be withdrawn gradually and the natural reinforcers will take over. Adult approval and doing a good job become established as conditioned reinforcers.

As already indicated, tokens are extremely effective in changing behavior. However, people rarely use tokens. One problem might be the expense of the programs. More likely, the problem is the complexity of many systems. We, therefore, recommend that people who use token systems keep them as simple as possible so that record keeping and the exchange system do not become cumbersome.

Basic Principles Quiz 4

1. Describe a behavior problem you are presently encountering. Devise a program to deal with the problem that makes use of tangible, activity, social, and token reinforcers.

2. Suppose the expression "Well done" is not a social reinforcer for someone. Indicate how you could make the expression into a social reinforcer.

3. Why is a gift certificate a less appealing reinforcer than money?

(*continues*)

4. Describe a token reinforcement system that would be relatively easy to implement.

5. Schools are already using a token reinforcement system—student grades. Why is the token system so often ineffective?

6. Compare the advantages and disadvantages of token systems with other reinforcement systems.

Selecting Appropriate Reinforcers

An important factor in a successful behavioral program is selecting an effective reinforcer. This can be achieved in several ways. One way is to ask people to identify effective reinforcers for their behavior. Admittedly, when people are asked to do this, they might request reinforcers that are prohibitively expensive or which are difficult to procure. By persevering in the process, however, it is possible to pinpoint effective and reasonable reinforcers.

A second way to identify potential reinforcers is to give the person a list of reinforcers and have him select from items and events on the list. When this is done, several potential reinforcers should be selected to allow for variety.

Another way to identify a potential reinforcer is to note what a person spends a lot of time doing. If someone spends a great deal of time in an activity, the activity is likely to be a reinforcer. Such events can then be made contingent on behavior and are likely to reinforce desired behaviors. For example, if an adult with a developmental disability spends a great deal of time watching television, this activity can be provided contingent on behaviors such as completing chores and socializing with others. If a youngster is found reading a comic book in English class, he can be awarded comic book reading time for completing his English assignment.

Finally, it is helpful to note what follows a behavior. A preschool child, who is consistently comforted after crying and continues crying, is probably reinforced by adult attention. An adult with developmental disabilities who runs from his living quarters to a fast-food restaurant is likely to work for the opportunity to go to the restaurant.

Several factors characterize a well-selected reinforcer. One factor is that the reinforcer is a naturally occurring consequence. That is, the reinforcer is one that is commonly present in a person's environment. Such reinforcers are often less costly and easier to arrange than contrived reinforcers. Thus, praise is a more natural reinforcer than posting a list of outstanding students, and a bonus in a paycheck is easier to provide than a trip to an exotic island.

The potential reinforcers listed here are consequent events that have been used successfully to increase the strength of behaviors of these varying populations. They may include reinforcers that can be used in the home, in school, or in working environments.

Natural reinforcers are more likely to continue to be available after the behavior has been established. If the reinforcers are natural to the situation, the person receiving them is more likely to come in contact with them in the natural environment after the systematic reinforcement program ends. Thus, a boy who has been rewarded for finishing his math assignment by being allowed time to read is more likely to continue to receive this reinforcement when he passes on to the next grade than if the original reinforcer had been candy or a toy.

(text continues on page 27)

Potential Reinforcers for Ages 0–4 at Home

Infant

Bright shiny objects
Rocking to sleep
Humming or singing
Moving or waving toy above crib
Change of diaper
Soft fuzzy toys
Smelling flower
Cooing
Finger paint
Taking a bath
Blanket
Tasting cake batter, soda, etc.
Riding in a stroller
Being tossed in air

Tangible

Toys
Snacks
Dessert
New shoes
Favorite food
Candy and other sweets
Drink of water, juice, etc.
Ice cream from truck

Activities

Trip to park
Playing with friends
Getting in bed with parents
Making mud pies
Bedtime story
Playing on swing set
Spending the night with friends or grandparents
Lifting into air
Opportunity to feed pet
Rocking
Games
Making noises (rattles, bells)
Swinging on foot (horsey ride)
Finger play
Taking a picture of how good they are
Playing with magnet
Talking into tape recorder
Eating out
Rocking in rocking chair
Wearing parent's clothing
Playing with clay
Going someplace along with Dad
Helping plan day's activities
Helping Mother or Dad
Longer time in bathtub
Riding on bicycle with Mom
Whirling in circle by arms
Special hour, day
Watching lightning
Playing in sandbox
Sitting in chair with parent
Not having to take bath one night
Blowing bubbles
Blowing out match
Popping balloon
Bouncing on bed
Playing outside
Riding tricycle
Staying up late
Trip to zoo
Piggyback ride
Bubble bath
Singing song
Sitting on lap
Whirling in chair
Flushing the toilet
Riding on Dad's shoulders
Going outside at night
Family night
Helping hold baby
Swimming
Being pulled in wagon
Carrying purse or briefcase

Social

Physical contact, hugs, kisses, tickles
Stroking under chin
Talking to child
Verbal praise
Winks
Eye contact
Smiling
Indirect praise, telling someone else how good they are

Tokens

Money
Stars on chart

(continues)

Potential Reinforcers for Ages 5–11 at Home

Tangible

Toys
Pets
Books

Snacks
Own bedroom
Clothing

Jigsaw puzzles

Activities

Dressing up in adult clothes
Trip to park
Playing with friends
Camping in backyard
Bedtime story
Playing on swing set
Spending night with friends or grandparents
Going to a ball game
Eating out
Going someplace alone with Dad
Baking something in kitchen
Planning a day's activities
Riding on bicycle
Fishing trip with Mom
Choice of television program
Freedom from chores
Holding hand while walking
Using telephone

Wearing parent's clothes
Setting the table
Opening coffee can, smelling aroma
Decorating home for holidays
Helping make dessert, popcorn, etc.
Helping take a gift to a friend
"Sit" for younger children while mother near
Feeding the baby
Late bedtime
Going to movies (especially with a friend)
Going alone on a trip by bus, plane, etc.
Holding nails while Dad hammers another
Playing favorite tapes and CDs

Coloring in coloring book
Riding next to window in car
Choosing menu for meal
Calling Grandma to tell of successes
Promising to ride escalator three or four times at the store
Displaying schoolwork on refrigerator door
Letting them buy something
Planting a garden
Playing with magnet
Playing with magnifying glass

Social

Hugs
Telling grandparents of accomplishments

Kisses
Handshake

Verbal praise

Tokens

Money
Stars on chart

Increase in allowance

Own bank account

(continues)

Potential Reinforcers for Ages 12–18 at Home

Tangible

Favorite meal
Clothes
Books
Radio
Bicycle
Electric razor, hair brush, dryer

Having own room
Having a soda
Television
Watch
Selecting own gift
Makeup (girls)
Private phone

Stereo
Jewelry
Guitar
CDs

Activities

Dating privileges
Participating in activities with friends
Having friends over
Dance or music lessons
Refrigerator privileges
Redecorating own room
Extended curfew
Car privileges
Staying up late
Staying overnight with friends
Time off from chores
Kidding and joking
Dating during week
Sewing own clothes

Watching television (choose program)
Camping out
Summer camp
Expensive haircut
Going to Disneyland with parents
Skating
Additional time on telephone
Playing stereo
Making trip alone on bus or plane
Choosing own bedtime
Part-time job
Car to school for a day

Getting driver's license
Reading
Opportunity to earn money
Selection of television program
Chairing family meeting
Getting to use family camera
Going to amusement park
Discussion with parents
Allow to sit alone when family eats out
Getting to sleep late on weekend

Social

Smiles
Attention when talking
Winks
Hugs

Being asked for opinion
Verbal praise
Head nods

"OK" gesture with thumb and finger
"V" sign

Tokens

Extra money
Having own checking account

Allowance
Driver's license
Magazine subscription

Gift certificate

(*continues*)

Potential Reinforcers for Elementary School Pupils

Tangible
Food

Activities
Recess (extra or longer)
Group leader
Going to library
Room "manager"
Hall monitor
Listening to records
Choosing song in music class
Individual conference on progress
Field trips
Sharpening pencil
Reading own composition to class
No homework
Choice of seat mate (for day, week, permanent)
Raise flag for day or week
Watch selves on videotape
Passing out milk
Having parents visit
Making gift for parent
Riding in seat behind bus driver
Playing instruments
Extra computer time
Crafts activities

Head of lunch line
Erasing boards
Going to principal's office
After school activity
Tutoring another pupil
Day to chew gum in class
Having picture taken
Leading class in singing
Picnics
Cafeteria helper
Displaying work to another class
Demonstrating hobby to class
Host in front hallway on parents' day
Going home early
Planning daily schedule
Colleting lunch tickets
Independent study
Principal's helper for day
Free activity corner in corner of room (puzzles, games)
Scheduling group, then individual activities
Performing before a group
Helping custodian

Fixing bulletin board
Running errands
First or last in line
Early dismissal
Playing game
Helping librarian
Viewing films
Party
Drink of water
Student government activity
Displaying work to principal
Making and viewing videotape
Team captain
Selecting bulletin board topic
Academic contests
Story time
Having lunch with teacher or principal
Scheduling quiet, then noisy activities
Time to lie on floor, sit on desk, study outside

Social
Smiles, winks
Verbal praise
Posting picture (student of month)
Principal praise
Being voted most improved student in academic area
Eye contact

Phone call to parents
Pat on back
Displaying self picture
Getting to time self with stopwatch
Homework (good papers) on bulletin board

Being on school patrol
Positive comments written on papers

Tokens
Badges to be worn for day signifying staff to give positive attention
Special certificate of completed work

Seeing progress toward going on picnic on graph
Points
Happy face on paper
Big red "C" on paper

Stars
Grades
Honor roll
Noting academic progress

(continues)

Potential Reinforcers for Secondary School Pupils

Tangible
Posters
Sports equipment
Music tapes
Magazines
Blank tapes
Paperback books
Ticket to show
Pizza, dried fruit
Nuts, pretzels, chips
Juice, soft drinks
Demo CDs

Activities
Having extra free time
Playing checkers, chess, or card game
Listening to private radio or tape
Having classroom party
Having day with no homework
Going on a field trip
Having extra gym time
Having extra lunch time
Working on computer
Teaching another student
Watching a tape
Having a class outside
Observing a science demonstration
Talking to another student
Playing cards

Social
Smiles, winks, handshakes
Victory sign, thumbs up
Pat on back
Complimentary phone call to student or parents
High achievement list
Private compliment
Honor roll
Complimentary note

Tokens
Increasing test grade
Increasing course grade
Point card with back-up reinforcers
Noting academic progress on chart
Gift certificate

Potential Reinforcers on the Job

Tangible
Prizes, television sets, stereos, carpeting, etc.
Small gifts (flowers for secretary)
Something to decorate office or work area
Special place to store personal belongings
Special parking space
Business card
Car allowance
Free coffee
Free lunch
Water cooler
More comfortable chair
Convert room for lounge
Personal mailbox
Larger office
Paid lunch allowance
Thermostat in office
Quiet area for break

Activities
Time off
Longer coffee breaks
Assisting someone with job
Trips (Hawaii, Bahamas)
Trips to conventions, workshops
Extra help on job
Choice of shift
Choice of location for work station
Reduced work load
Promotion to better job
Having lunch, vacation with boss
Transfer request accepted
Access to secretarial help
Piped in music
Parties, social events
Day off for birthday
Coming in late for having worked extra hours
Private office

(continues)

Potential Reinforcers on the Job *(Continued)*

Activities *(Continued)*

Tenure or other evidence of job security
Not having to "punch" clock
Leaving five minutes early
Lunch on the boss
Added responsibilities

Extra vacation
Personal business time off
Supervising trainee
Being able to take spouse to convention, or not being required to take spouse to convention

Paid for continuing education
Voice in decision making
Invitation to participate in special project

Social

Verbal praise from supervisor
Group recognition for achievement
Eye contact
Employee of week, month, year
New title

Recognition for suggestions
Special job title
Note of appreciation
Picture or name in company paper
Listening to suggestions
Posting production charts
Praise from peers

Good work evaluation
Name on desk or office door
Greeting from boss
Asking person to explain his work to visitors

Tokens

Merit salary increase
Certificate of outstanding performance
Bonus

Points backed by prizes
Free tickets to recreation or social event

Telephone credit card

Potential Reinforcers for Spouses/Significant Others

Tangible

Clothes
Flowers
Making breakfast in bed

Jewelry
Special cards
Magazine subscription

Furniture
Car
Perfume/cologne

Activities

Going out to eat
Telephone call during day
Going dancing
Time to talk
Time off from household responsibilities
Night out alone
Being warned when in-laws are coming

Choosing side of bed to sleep on
Going grocery shopping together
Having hair brushed
Baby-sitting
Massage
Remembering important occasions

Surprise party
Weekend away from kids
Sleeping late on weekends
Time alone
Consulting about important decisions
Chance to select movie
Attention in public

(continues)

Potential Reinforcers for Spouses/Significant Others *(Continued)*

Social

Compliments in presence of another person	Compliments on appearance	Eye contact
Verbal praise, compliments	Pet name	Saying "I love you"
Smiles	Positive feedback on household jobs	Romantic dialogue
Listening intently	Back rubs, hugs, kisses, and other physical contact	No mention of past mistakes
Being on time for dinner		Phone call

Tokens

Extra money	Memberships	Gift Certificate

People should always strive to bring the persons with whom they work in contact with natural reinforcers to maintain the behavior. People should attempt to arrange or rearrange the reinforcers occurring naturally in the environment to their advantage. If reinforcers have been presented in the past on a noncontingent basis, they have gone to waste. Even worse, the person of concern has developed patterns of behavior that will make her less likely to come in contact with all the reinforcers, which would otherwise be available.

One mother was concerned about her four-year-old son, who took more than two hours to dress himself in the morning. He preferred to watch television and would not dress quickly unless she scolded him severely, spanked him, or dressed him herself. She instituted a program in which watching television was contingent on getting dressed within 10 minutes of getting out of bed each morning. As a result, her son came into contact with a number of reinforcers that had not been available before. He still got to see his favorite television programs, and he received praise from his mother and father for his behavior. Nagging, spanking, and other unpleasant actions were avoided. In addition, the son's opinion of himself changed. He told his grandmother that he was no longer a baby because he got up and got dressed on time by himself.

Another characteristic of a reinforcer that will enhance its effectiveness is novelty. People can be very motivated to work for a surprise. The surprise reinforcer can be intermingled with a predictable, but desirable, reinforcer. Therefore, it is important to become skilled at selecting new and different reinforcers to maintain high behavior rates.

A potential reinforcer may be ineffective because a person has never experienced it. In such cases one can use a *reinforcer sampling* procedure in which a person engages in the reinforcing event for a short period of time before being required to earn it. Car salespeople take advantage of this process when they have potential customers sample a new car over the weekend. If a teacher wants to use a game such as Seven Up as a reinforcer, and the students are not familiar with the game, she can have the children play the game for five minutes before they are required to work for it.

▶ **Assignment:** Use three different ways to identify a reinforcer for the following people:

1. A child
2. An adult
3. Yourself

Basic Principles Quiz 5

Fred was a 17-year-old junior in high school. He frequently skipped classes and was receiving D's and F's except for gym. He was also argumentative at home. He frequently shouted at his parents and claimed that they did not give him enough allowance or access to the car even though his parents owned two cars. He also objected because his mother nagged him about school, keeping his room clean, and coming in on time. The school counselor had tried setting up a program whereby Fred could earn privileges, such as going to assemblies or visiting the student lounge, for going to class or getting good grades. However, Fred had not responded but instead continued to skip classes except for gym. He frequently disappeared to play arcade games at a shopping center or basketball at an outdoor court in a nearby playground.

1. Why did the school counselor's program fail?

_____

_____

_____

_____

_____

_____

_____

Behavior Modification: Basic Principles

2. Fred's program suggests that certain activities might be reinforcers for him. What are they?

3. Select one of Fred's behaviors and suggest a contingency you think might be effective in changing it.

4. Suggest a reinforcer sampling procedure the parents might use in order to increase the probability that Fred will respond to a reinforcer they might offer.

Applying Reinforcement

Contingency Contracting

In some situations a person such as a parent, teacher, or employer embarks on a program to change the behavior of a child, student, or employee. Although most human interactions proceed quite naturally in this way, some people object to the arrangement because they see it as coercive and controlling. Some people believe that all parties should first agree to a behavior-change program before it proceeds. Such people might also claim that if a person agrees to have his behavior modified, he is more likely to participate in the program and to show behavioral gains. One manner of achieving these ends is through a *contingency contract*. A contingency contract is a written agreement between at least two parties that specifies the reinforcers one party will present if the other party meets specified goals. The agreement can be between an employer and employee, between a teacher, a parent, and a student, or may take many other forms. Some contracts also specify bonuses for outstanding performance and penalties for inappropriate behaviors. The explicit, written form of a contract makes contingencies clear and helps all parties meet their responsibilities. As the word *contract* implies, the terms of the agreement should involve negotiation between all parties and should specify an expiration date or the terms under which the contract can be renegotiated (e.g., one party's unhappiness with it). On the following page is a contract written between a nine-year-old boy and his mother.

Writing effective contracts involves following several guidelines. First of all, contracts should specify the positive rather than the negative—that is, they should emphasize what a person can achieve for meeting the terms of the contract, rather than penalties for not meeting behavioral criteria. The contract should provide small reinforcers for reasonable improvement, rather than large rewards for unrealistic gains. Contracts should also provide for short-term rather than long-term reinforcers. Also, the terms of the contract should be clear to all parties. Lastly, as progress occurs, the contract should be gradually adjusted with more terms being determined by the person whose behavior is being altered.

▶ **Assignment:** Suggest a contingency contract for one of the following:

a) parent and teenager, b) teacher, parent, and student,
c) domestic partners, d) employer and employee

_____

_____

Contingency Contract

We agree that whenever Hector puts away his toys at the end of the day and takes out the trash when requested, he will receive one point. When he receives five points he will be allowed to have a friend sleep over on the weekend or go to a movie of his choosing.

April 3	Hector Wright
Date	Hector's signature

April 17	Virginia Wright
Expiration Date	Mother's signature

_____

_____

_____

_____

_____

_____

Opportunities To Respond and Three-Term Contingencies

People learn new behaviors by getting chances to respond and receiving feedback as to whether their responses were appropriate or not. This unit of instruction is known as the *three-term contingency*. In a classroom this might consist of a teacher asking a question (first term), the students responding (second term), and the teacher giving the students feedback on their answers (third term). Unfortunately, too few teaching arrangements allow for the use of three-term contingencies. A visitor to a classroom might see one student reading aloud and the others staring into space or getting into trouble. A parent or supervisor might tell a child or employee how to perform a task, but not provide the person with an opportunity to perform the behavior or give feedback as to how well the task was done.

If three-term contingencies are important in the learning process, how can they be provided? One way is through one-to-one tutoring programs, when one person who is competent at a skill teaches another person who has not yet mastered the skill. A second is through classwide peer tutoring, in which all students take turns being tutor and learner. Another is through choral responding, in which a teacher asks a question, the group responds on a signal, and the teacher gives the students feedback on their answers. Also, response cards are helpful (Heward et al., 1996). The teacher asks a question, the students write their answers on an erasable board, and the teacher provides feedback. Finally, computer-assisted instruction programs provide users with many opportunities to respond and offer immediate feedback on answers.

▶ **Assignment:** Devise a program by which one of the following can use more three-term contingencies:

a) an employer and employee, b) a teacher and a student, or c) a parent and a child

Teaching New Behaviors Through Shaping

It is easy to see how a reinforcement procedure can increase the occurrence of a behavior that already exists. If a secretary occasionally proofreads her work and her boss offers her a bonus for improved performance, she is likely to proofread at a higher rate. How reinforcement can be used to teach a new behavior is less obvious, because one cannot reinforce a behavior that does not already exist. Fortunately, through a process known as *shaping*, reinforcement can be used to teach a new behavior.

Shaping takes advantage of the fact that almost any behavior occurs with variability—that is, it sometimes occurs one way, it next occurs in a slightly different way, and then occurs in a third way. Shaping consists of reinforcing the existing behavior that comes closest to the desired (or *terminal*) behavior and then reinforcing closer and closer approximations to the terminal behavior. Once the terminal behavior is performed, it is reinforced until it reliably occurs. The behavior that is reinforced at the end is very different from the behavior that is reinforced at the beginning. This process is also known as reinforcing *successive approximations* of the desired behavior.

A mother who is trying to teach her young son to say "Ma Ma" provides an example of the shaping process. In the beginning, any sound is reinforced. Later, a verbalization is reinforced only if it has the sound "m" in it. Next, "Ma" is reinforced, and still later it must be an intelligible "Ma Ma." Sometimes shaping occurs naturally, such as learning to shift gears in a car with a standard transmission. A person's shifting behavior becomes more and more dexterous in order to avoid unpleasant sounds and a bucking sensation. Shaping a behavior is the ultimate skill in the teaching process. Shaping can be achieved by following certain rules:

1. Define the terminal behavior.
2. Determine the initial behavior that the person can already perform (i.e., the closest approximation to the terminal behavior).
3. Break the target behavior into graduated steps, beginning with the behavior the person can already perform and ending with the terminal behavior.
4. Have the person perform each step, reinforcing each one as it is achieved.
5. If a step is not performed, go back to an easier step until it is performed or further divide the existing steps into smaller steps.
6. Continue the procedure until the person is reliably performing the terminal behavior.

A person is likely to encounter two main difficulties in shaping a new behavior. One difficulty is caused by moving in steps that are too large. Thus, the difference between one step in the shaping process and the next step should be small. The idea is to challenge someone but not to frustrate her. The second difficulty is not providing enough practice at a newly learned step before moving on to the next step. In teaching a new mathematical operation, for example, as students are giving evidence of mastery, the teacher should provide a great deal of practice before moving to the next step.

▶ **Assignments:**

1. Suggest a shaping procedure for a student who could only sit still for two minutes in an hour. The desired terminal behavior is to sit still for 55 minutes an hour.

_____

_____

_____

_____

_____

2. Suggest a shaping procedure for behavior you wish to learn and implement the procedure. Report the results of your efforts.

_____

_____

_____

_____

_____

Schedules of Reinforcement

A schedule of reinforcement is the pattern of timing by which reinforcers are delivered. So far we have described reinforcement as if it were delivered each time an appropriate behavior was emitted. When this is the case, a *continuous reinforcement schedule* is in effect. Of course, it is not always possible, or even desirable, to reinforce every appropriate behavior. An alternative is to use an *intermittent* or *partial reinforcement schedule,* in which only a portion of the behaviors is reinforced. Continuous reinforcement schedules produce the fastest learning, whereas intermittent schedules produce the most durable behavior. Thus, it is advisable to start training with a continuous or near continuous schedule and end training with an intermittent schedule.

Intermittent Schedules of Reinforcement

Although there are numerous schedules of reinforcement, four are commonly used. Two are ratio schedules and two are interval schedules.

Ratio Schedules

Reinforcement in ratio schedules is delivered contingent on the number of responses a person has emitted. There are two types of ratio schedules: fixed and variable.

Fixed-ratio (FR) schedules

This schedule designates the exact number of behaviors a person must perform in order to receive a reinforcer. On an FR 10 (i.e., fixed ratio of 10 responses) schedule, for example, a reinforcer is delivered after 10 correct behaviors occur. Thus, a teacher can offer a student a minute of free time for every 10 math problems he gets right. FR schedules produce high, steady rates of performance once responding starts. After a reinforcer, however, a *post-reinforcement pause* usually occurs, after which responding begins again. Piecework is an example of fixed ratio responding. For example, an apple picker works rapidly once he begins picking apples, but he pauses after the box is full. Then he picks rapidly until the next box is filled, and so forth. A cumulative graph shows the total number of FR responses since the beginning of the study (see Figure 1).

Variable-ratio (VR) schedules

VR schedules specify the *average* number of responses a person must make to achieve reinforcement. On a VR 10 schedule, an average of 1 out of 10 responses is reinforced; the actual number of responses will vary from one

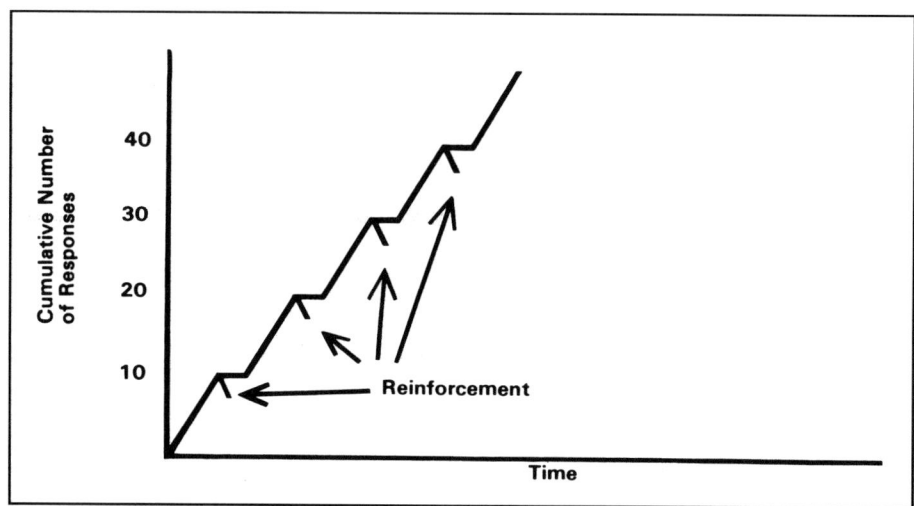

FIGURE 1. Fixed ratio reinforcement.

reinforcer to the next. On a VR 10 schedule, 2, 14, 7, 13, 18, and 6 responses can separate reinforcers. (Note that the average of these numbers is 10.) VR schedules tend to produce high, steady rates of performance and usually are not characterized by the post-reinforcement pauses associated with FR schedules. Examples of VR schedules include almost any field of sales where a variable number of attempts are reinforced and blind dates, which are said to be on a large VR schedule. A cumulative record of typical VR responding is displayed in Figure 2.

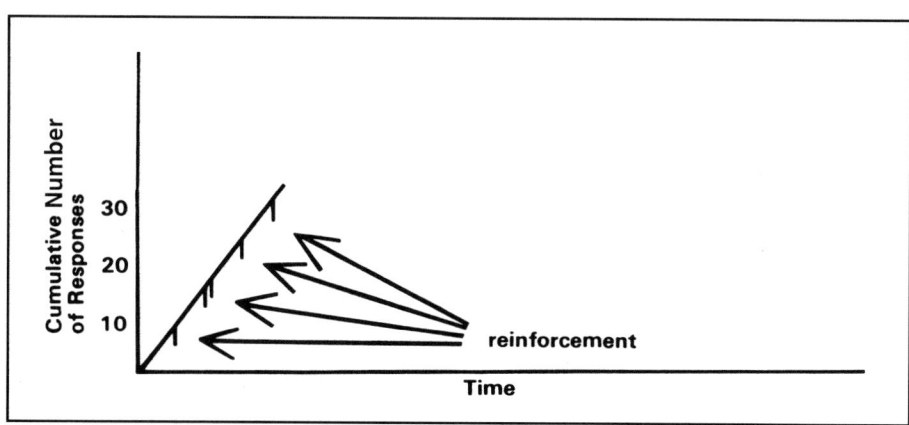

FIGURE 2. Variable ratio reinforcement.

Interval Schedules

With interval schedules, the first behavior to be emitted after a certain amount of time passes is reinforced. There are two types of interval schedules: fixed and variable.

Fixed-interval (FI) schedules

FI schedules specify the *exact* amount of time that must pass before a behavior is reinforced. FI 7 schedule means that seven minutes must pass before the specified behavior is reinforced. The pattern of responding that emerges from an FI schedule consists of very little responding at the beginning of an interval, followed by a burst of activity at the end of the interval. The behavior of members of Congress is on an FI schedule, since few bills are passed at the beginning of a session and many are passed at the end of a session, with re-election looming. Similarly, college students are known to do most of their studying just before examinations. Figure 3 shows a cumulative record of FI responding.

An example of FI 24 hr. responding can be seen in a person who is expecting an important letter. The rate of checking the mailbox increases greatly just before the mail carrier arrives. After the mail arrives the behavior ceases abruptly for almost 24 hours, then increases once again just before the mail carrier's next scheduled arrival.

Variable-interval (VI) schedules

A VI schedule specifies the *average* amount of time that must pass before a behavior is reinforced. The actual amount of time will vary from one behavior to the next. Thus, a VI 7 schedule could program reinforcement 3, 12, 9, 2, 5, 11 minutes apart. (Note that the average of the above numbers is 7.) VI schedules produce steady and moderate rates of response. The response rate

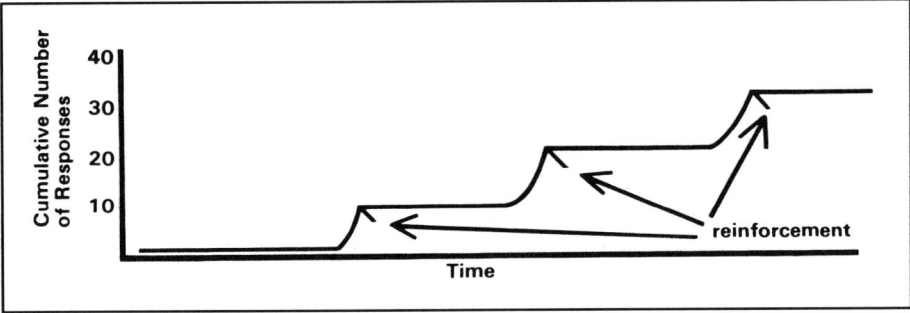

FIGURE 3. Fixed interval schedule.

38 Behavior Modification: Basic Principles

is higher than that generated by FI schedules, but not as high as ratio schedules. The game of *Musical Chairs* is on a VI schedule and the participants maintain a steady rate of alertness. Pop quizzes, another example of VI schedules, keep students studying at a steady, but not frantic, rate. Figure 4 illustrates a cumulative record of VI responding.

After the required amount of time has passed on both FI and VI schedules, a person must then perform a behavior to achieve a reinforcer. A reinforcer is not delivered simply based on the passage of time. The following comparison in Figure 5 of how the various schedules are displayed will help the reader to distinguish the schedules from each other.

The following facts may help people remember which schedules produce which effects:

Ratio schedules = high rates

Interval schedules = low rates

Fixed schedules = pauses

Variable schedules = steady responding

These facts can be combined to reveal that FI schedules produce low rates of response with pauses, and VR schedules produce steady and high rates, and so forth.

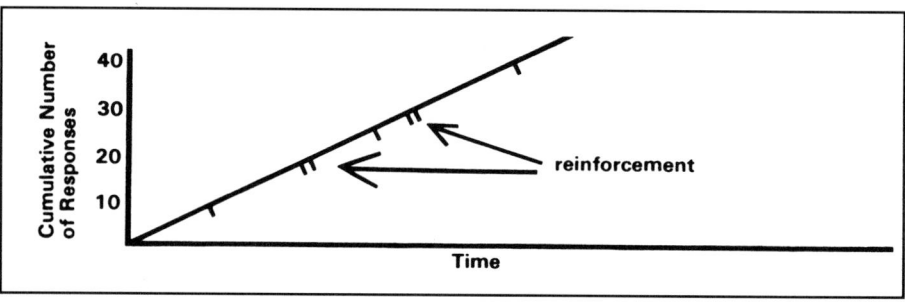

FIGURE 4. Variable interval schedule.

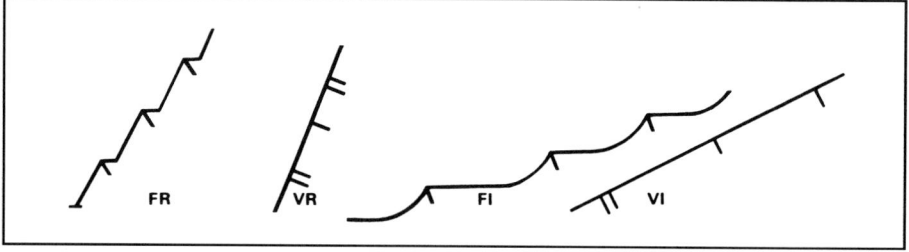

FIGURE 5. Comparison of reinforcement schedules.

Feedback

When a reinforcer is delivered, two functions are served. The first and more obvious function is that the reinforcer motivates the person to continue performing the behavior. The second function is informing the person that he performed the behavior correctly. The latter function is *feedback* and refers to information on the quality or quantity of past performance. Evidence supports that feedback alone can sometimes improve a person's behavior (Van Houten, 1980). We have found, for example, that handing a student teacher a note, indicating how many times she used three-term contingencies, can markedly improve her rate. Also, a public graph of how many new calls a salesperson made or how many times a person engaged in aerobic exercise in a week can result in substantial improvement. The significant point here is that information alone is sometimes sufficient for change. Expensive and unwieldy reinforcers are not always necessary.

Basic Principles Quiz 6

1. What is a contingency contract? What are some rules for a well-written contract?

   _____

   _____

   _____

   _____

   _____

2. What is a three-term contingency? Describe an interaction between a teacher and student that qualifies as a three-term contingency. Describe one that does not.

   _____

   _____

   _____

   _____

   _____

(continues)

3. Describe a behavior that does not exist in someone's repertoire and list the steps you would use to shape the behavior.

4. Why would it be best to use a continuous reinforcement schedule in shaping a new behavior?

(*continues*)

5. Why do ratio schedules produce higher rates of response than interval schedules?

_____

_____

_____

_____

6. Once a behavior is established, what kind of reinforcement schedule should be used to maintain the behavior? Why?

_____

_____

_____

_____

7. Give an example as to how reinforcement might be arranged on a VR 15 schedule.

_____

_____

_____

_____

Procedures for Decreasing Behavior

Until now, we have discussed reinforcement procedures and how they can be used to get existing behaviors to occur more frequently or to create new behaviors where a need exists. Sometimes, however, people are faced with unacceptable behaviors and need to find procedures that will decrease their occurrence. Examples of this behavior include a boy who frequently hits his sister, a student who teases a classmate, and an employer who publicly reprimands her workers. We will now discuss procedures that can be used to decrease or eliminate unacceptable behavior.

Decreasing Behavior Through Extinction

Sometimes an inappropriate behavior has been frequently reinforced in the past. For example, a mother may have reinforced her son's whining by giving the child what he wanted; or a teacher may have reinforced a student's profanity by showing that he was upset. In these cases a person can cease reinforcing the behavior and may find that the behavior occurs less frequently. *When the reinforcement for a behavior is terminated and the behavior decreases to low rates, extinction has taken place.* Such processes are common in our environment. People will stop working if they are not paid and will stop patronizing a sports team that seldom wins. Often the process consists of planned ignoring of inappropriate behavior.

People trying to achieve extinction of a behavior should go through the following steps:

1. Define the target behavior and obtain a Baseline on its occurrence.

2. Observe the consequences of the behavior to determine what might be reinforcing the behavior.

3. Arrange for the removal of the reinforcing consequences (e.g., ignore the behavior).

4. Continue to record the occurrence of the behavior to see if it decreases to low rates.

The above statements notwithstanding, extinction is not always easy to achieve. The process is typically slow acting. The speed of the process can be increased when used in conjunction with the reinforcement of a desirable behavior—that is, if a parent is no longer attending to a child's whining, she can reinforce requests made in a pleasant manner. A teacher who is no longer showing that he is upset by a student's profanity can praise the youngster when he speaks properly.

In addition to being a slow acting process, a number of other problems exist. First, most people find it difficult not to react to inappropriate behavior. In addition, even if one person stops reacting to a problem, it is possible that other people will continue to reinforce the behavior. Also, a behavior undergoing extinction may occur more frequently before it decreases in rate. This process is known as *extinction burst* and may prove intolerable to some people who, consequently, will then weaken and reinforce the behavior. In addition, behaviors that have decreased in rate tend to suddenly recur. *Spontaneous recovery* of the behavior might prove troublesome for people who are not prepared for it. Another problem is that the person whose behavior is being ignored might respond with aggression, crying, or frustration. Finally, some behaviors, such as self-injury or property destruction, are too dangerous or expensive to ignore.

In spite of these problems, the process has some benefits and can be used under carefully controlled conditions. For example, the process could be used with a child who cries for attention every night when put to sleep. This application involves few dangers and it usually works after a few nights. Also, the process has the advantage of not programming any unpleasant consequences that occur with punishment procedures. Finally, the procedure provides the motivation for creativity. When a person's key no longer opens a door, for example, she is motivated to look for alternative means of entry.

Resistance to extinction is the number of behaviors a person performs after reinforcement is terminated. It may be surprising to learn that behaviors on an intermittent schedule of reinforcement will show more resistance to extinction (i.e., will extinguish more slowly) than behaviors on a continuous reinforcement schedule. For example, people will more quickly stop using a vending machine that doesn't work than a slot machine that is broken. Also, variable schedules of reinforcement produce more resistance to extinction than fixed schedules, due to the unpredictability of reinforcement on variable schedules. An extinction curve usually looks something like the one of a boy who engaged in frequent tantrums until his parents began to systematically ignore tantrums, as shown in Figure 6.

When extinction begins there is usually a sharp burst of increased behavior, which lasts for a relatively short time, and then a sharp decrease to lower levels. The rate at which extinction occurs depends on the kind of reinforcement schedule used. Because of the extinction curve (an increase and then a sharp decrease), it is extremely important for persons using this procedure to record the behavior. Parents who see the behavior record change as predicted are much more likely to carry through than if left to their own devices. This is especially true if their son or daughter is very skilled at getting attention by crying, screaming, kicking, coughing, and so forth, with increasing intensity because of a history of having been reinforced for doing so by the well-meaning but distraught parents.

> ▶ **Question:** Each time Marsha cries after being put to bed, her parents come to her room, comfort her, and get her a drink of water. Tony's parents, on the other hand, often go to him when he cries, but sometimes they let him cry a long time before they respond to him. On some nights they let him "cry it out" without ever going to him. One night, both sets of parents decide that they will henceforth let the children cry until they fall asleep. Other things being equal, which child will become a good sleeper first? Why?

44 Behavior Modification: Basic Principles

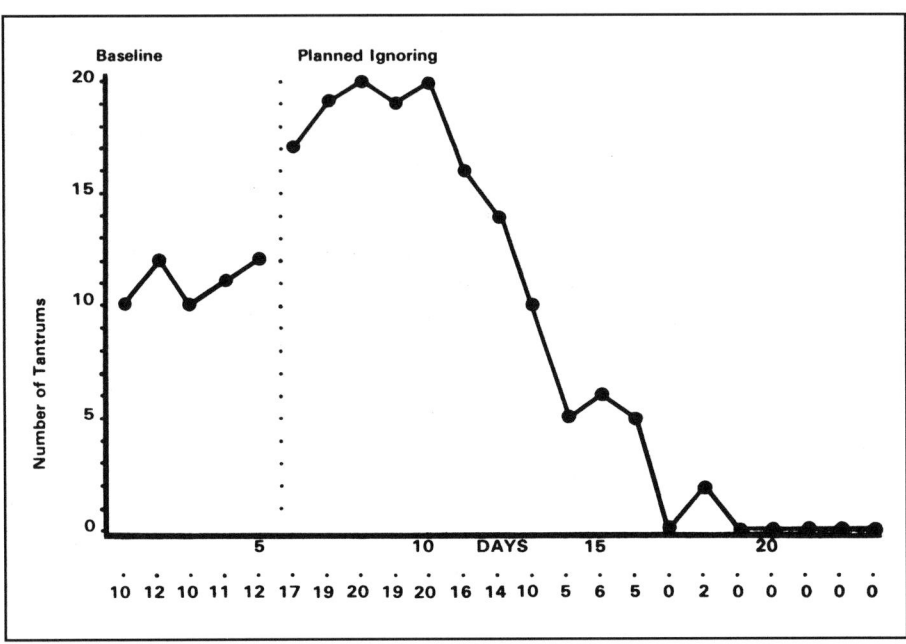

FIGURE 6. Typical extinction curve.

(continues)

Decreasing Behavior Through Reinforcement

Because reinforcement was previously described as a means to increase behavior, it might seem surprising that it is also a means of decreasing behavior. Yet, there are some ways in which reinforcement can be used in this manner. One procedure, known as *differential reinforcement of low rate of response (DRL)*, provides reinforcement to an individual or a group when the behavior occurs below a specified level. For example, a father might allow his daughter to stay up an extra 15 minutes if she leaves less than four items of clothing on the floor on a given day. A teacher might inform her students that they can watch a tape if they perform less than 20 out-of-seat behaviors in a morning. As the behavior of the children improves, the criterion can be gradually reduced to 18, 15, 12, and so forth.

A second means of decreasing behavior through reinforcement is to use a *differential reinforcement of other (DRO) schedule of reinforcement*. With this schedule a reinforcer is delivered if a specified behavior does not occur for a stated period of time. Suppose a child frequently sucks her thumb. On a DRO 10 schedule, she would receive a reinforcer if she refrained from sucking her thumb for 10 minutes. A new 10-minute cycle would then begin. If she sucked her thumb before 10 minutes passed, the timer would be reset and a new 10-minute (or greater in some cases) cycle would begin.

A third way of reducing behavior through reinforcement is by *reinforcing an incompatible behavior*. For example, if an employee is often late, he can be praised or receive a complimentary note when he is punctual. In a classroom, the best way to reinforce incompatible behavior is to use a large number of three-term contingencies as described earlier. When students are fully occupied by responding correctly to academic tasks, they simply cannot misbehave.

> ▶ **Assignment:** Identify an inappropriate behavior exhibited by an employee, domestic partner, or child and use one of the reinforcement procedures described in this section to reduce it.

Decreasing Behavior Through Punishment

Unfortunately, ignoring behavior and reinforcement procedures does not always produce desirable reduction in unacceptable behavior. An effective but controversial means of reducing behavior is to use punishment procedures. A *punisher* is defined as any consequence of behavior that reduces the future rate of that behavior (Azrin & Holz, 1966). Suppose a student has been taunting another child 15 times daily. If the teacher requires the student to sit in a corner of the room for five minutes each time the behavior occurs, and the rate decreases to lower rates, punishment has occurred. If the rate stays the same or gets higher, punishment has not occurred.

Punishment is not the same as negative reinforcement. In the case of negative reinforcement, a person responds at a high rate to avoid or escape an unpleasant event. With punishment a person responds less frequently to avoid the unpleasant event. Negative reinforcement produces an increase in behavior. Punishment produces a decrease in behavior.

Research has revealed that several factors influence the use of punishment procedures (Azrin & Holz, 1966). First, the more intense the punisher is, the more effective the punishment is. Also, it is better to use an intense punisher at the start and gradually reduce its intensity than to proceed in the opposite manner (which unfortunately is the common tendency). Also, if people can avoid punishment through apologies, lies, or "one more chance," the punishment procedure will be ineffective. The most important method is to combine reinforcement of appropriate behavior with punishment for inappropriate behavior. If a person is reprimanded for absenteeism, she should be complimented for coming to work. If a child is required to go to sleep early for breaking her younger brother's toys, she should receive reinforcement when she treats his toys properly. The reinforcement component teaches the correct behavior and results in a quicker and greater reduction in the undesirable behavior. It also allows one to use a less intense punisher and still be effective.

One of the major concerns about punishment techniques is that they can result in undesirable side effects. Indeed, research has sometimes found this to be true (Newsom, Favell, & Rincover, 1983). Undesirable side effects can involve aggression toward the person administering punishment or toward others in the environment (i.e., scapegoating). A person receiving punishment might cry, scream, or pout. She might also try to entirely avoid the person or environment where punishment occurs (e.g., by "playing hooky"). Such occurrences are relatively rare and can be averted by the previously mentioned action of combining positive reinforcement for appropriate behavior with punishment for inappropriate behavior.

As indicated earlier, the use of punishment techniques has been widely criticized. Some researchers (e.g., La Vigna & Donnellan, 1986) claim that only positive techniques should be used in behavior change. One issue, however, is that the natural environment automatically punishes some behaviors. This type of punishment occurs when we walk into walls or put our hands in boiling water. Still, the question remains as to whether teachers, employers, and parents should *program* punishment. Probably, this is sometimes necessary. Indeed, people who claim that others should not use punishment procedures engage in fierce attacks on those who do. The best way to proceed is to use frequent positive reinforcement, but also to occasionally use properly applied punishment. The next section discusses three punishment techniques that can be helpful and humanely employed.

Some Effective Punishment Procedures

Reprimands

A common and acceptable form of punishment is the reprimand. A reprimand is any expression of disapproval and can consist of verbal disapproval, a pointed finger, or a critical facial guise (Van Houten & Doleys, 1983). Combining two or more forms of reprimands is generally more effective than using only one. Reprimands are easy to deliver and do not involve pain or discomfort to the recipient. Examples of reprimands include a father telling his son, "Don't talk to your sister that way"; a teacher telling a class to "Keep quiet"; or an employer admonishing an employee to stop coming to work late. Verbal reprimands should be delivered right after a behavior occurs, should be delivered privately whenever possible, should be brief, and should be delivered while making eye contact. Verbal reprimands should specify the undesirable behavior and should not demean the recipient's character. Thus, it is more humane to say, "What you just did was inconsiderate," rather than, "You are inconsiderate." Reprimands for inappropriate behavior should be combined with praise for appropriate behavior.

Response Cost

A powerful and socially acceptable form of punishment is response cost. The procedure involves removing certain amounts of a person's or group's reinforcers following an unacceptable behavior. Reinforcers that can be removed include tokens, free time, money, points, and so forth. Response cost is often carried out in conjunction with a token reinforcement program. In one form of response cost, people are given free reinforcers and can lose them contingent on each undesirable behavior. In a second form of response cost, people can earn reinforcers for correct behavior and lose reinforcers for incorrect behavior. The popular television quiz show *Jeopardy* is an example of the second type of response-cost procedure.

There are numerous examples of response cost in our environment. When the government fines its citizens for a traffic violation, it is using a response-cost procedure. The same is true for the telephone company when it charges customers for making directory-assisted calls that exceed a specified limit. A supermarket that removes shortages from a cashier's paycheck is also using response cost.

Parents can also use response cost. A child can be offered 10 extra minutes of staying-up time each night. Each time he teases his sister, however, he loses two minutes of the extra time. If he has no extra minutes left, the child can then be required to go to sleep two minutes earlier than usual for each additional misbehavior.

Teachers can also make use of response-cost procedures. One of the most powerful procedures we have encountered is the use of response cost with an entire group of students. For example, a teacher offers her students 12 extra minutes of free time. She writes the number of minutes on the chalkboard in this form:

12 11 10 9 8 7 6 5 4 3 2 1 0

Each time a student breaks a specified rule (e.g., leaving his seat without permission), the entire group loses a minute of free time. Thus, if three rules were broken, the teacher would mark off three minutes on the board:

1̷2 1̷1 1̷0 9 8 7 6 5 4 3 2 1 0

When the time is over, the group gets the amount of free time that remains. In this case, three rules were broken and, thus, nine minutes of free time remain.

Response cost can also be used to improve an academic skill. Students, for example, can earn a point for each problem done correctly and lose a point for each error. The points left over can be used to purchase back-up reinforcers. A college professor once devised a means for preventing some students from dominating classroom discussions. Each student started the day with three markers and was required to remove a marker for each question she asked. When she used up her three markers, her contributions to the class were over.

The advantages of response-cost procedures are that they are easy to apply, often produce immediate and major decreases in inappropriate behavior, and produce long-lasting effects. The disadvantages of response cost are that sometimes people become upset when they lose a reinforcer, that people "give up" when all their reinforcers are gone, and that too much attention is given to inappropriate behavior. To combat the last problem, people using response cost should compliment appropriate behavior when it occurs.

Time Out

A third form of punishment that is sometimes more controversial than the first two forms is known as *time out from positive reinforcement,* or more commonly as *time out.* The procedure involves having a person experience a less reinforcing environment for a period of time following an inappropriate behavior. According to this broad definition, the existing environment can be made less reinforcing by, for example, removing a personal radio for 10 minutes; or, the person can be removed from the present environment and placed in a less appealing one, such as an empty room.

Time-out procedures are commonly used in our environment. In athletics, for example, coaches will take players out of a game for several minutes for poor play. In ice hockey, players are required to sit in the penalty box for a period of time for breaking a rule. In home situations, a parent will frequently require a child to sit in a corner of the house for a few minutes following an unacceptable behavior. A student who throws food or pushes schoolmates in the cafeteria might be required to spend the rest of the lunch period sitting by himself.

Schools have sometimes made formal use of time-out procedures. In one arrangement, known as *contingent observation,* a student must sit in a corner of the classroom for a period of time, but can observe and participate in classroom assignments. In a second arrangement, *exclusion time out,* the student faces the corner of the room for a specified period of time, but cannot participate in any classroom activities. In the third arrangement, *seclusion time out,* the student is isolated from other people in the school in a barren room for a period of time.

Three matters concerning time out merit attention. First, time out will be effective only to the extent that the normal (i.e., time-in) environment is more reinforcing than the time-out environment. Thus, putting a student in a hallway might be ineffective if the hallway is more fun than the classroom. Parents should not be surprised if sending a child to his room is an ineffective procedure if the child's room contains diversions such as a CD player, a television, and a telephone. (Prohibiting the use of these devices during time out might be helpful.)

A second issue is that the purpose of time out is to punish inappropriate behavior. It is not a time to counsel or console a person. The purpose of a time-out procedure is to deprive a person of her usual reinforcers, not to provide new ones.

Finally, seclusion time out, when used in education, is seen by many people as an extreme procedure. Therefore, it should not be used until reasonable alternatives have been ruled out, unless school district policies are carefully followed, and all relevant parties agree to the necessity and nature of the time-out procedure. This discussion should include parents, the teacher, and the school's principal.

Basic Principles Quiz 7

1. Mark is a child who constantly irritates his mother until she gets angry with him. Mom suspects that the attention she gives to Mark is reinforcing the behavior. Therefore, she will try to extinguish the behavior by ignoring Mark's irritating comments. What are three things that Mark's mother should expect to happen?

   _____

   _____

   _____

   _____

   _____

   _____

   _____

2. What is resistance to extinction? Which schedule of reinforcement should produce the greatest resistance to extinction?

   _____

   _____

   _____

   _____

   _____

   _____

(continues)

3. What is a DRL schedule of reinforcement? Suppose you wished to reduce out-of-seat behaviors in a classroom. How would you use DRL? Indicate how you would set the original criterion for reinforcement and how you would lower it.

4. Define extinction and punishment. How are extinction and punishment alike? How are they different?

5. How are negative reinforcement and punishment different? Give an example of each procedure.

6. Describe three factors that would make a punishment procedure more effective.

(continues)

7. When punishing an inappropriate behavior, why is it also important to reinforce an appropriate behavior? Describe a program that does this.

8. Describe the conditions under which you would use a punishment procedure.

Antecedents of Behavior

So far we have emphasized the manner in which events that follow a behavior affect the future rate of that behavior. These events are consequent events and may be reinforcing or punishing. Events that precede a behavior also affect its occurrence. These events are called *antecedent stimuli* and also have a major effect on behavior. Thus, some parents will call their children in for dinner and the children immediately come into the kitchen (we've been told). The school bell rings and students immediately grab their belongings and line up for dismissal. Bosses ask secretaries to proofread their work and many do as they are told. Looking at the antecedents and consequences of behavior is often referred to as the *ABCs of behavior.*

Stimulus Control

Most antecedent events have no natural power to produce behavior. These initially neutral stimuli, however, can come to have profound effects on our behavior because of the way they are paired with stimulus consequences (i.e., reinforcers or punishers). Some stimuli act as cues for us to emit certain behaviors. These cues are called *discriminative stimuli (S^Ds).* They inform us that, if we make certain responses in their presence, reinforcement is likely to follow. Other stimuli, which do not signal reinforcement for a behavior, are called *nondiscriminative stimuli (S^Δs or S deltas).* They tell us not to emit those responses in their presence.

The process of teaching someone to make a discrimination between an S^D and an S^Δ is called *differential reinforcement.* This means that people consistently reinforce a behavior in the presence of a certain S^D. People never reinforce it in the presence of other stimuli (S^Δ). Soon it is apparent that the behavior is emitted only in the presence of the S^D and not the S^Δ.

S^D → Response → Reinforcement → S^D → Response → Reinforcement

S^Δ → Response → No Reinforcement → S^Δ → No Response

When a behavior reliably occurs in the presence of one stimulus, but does not occur in its absence, the behavior is said to be under *stimulus control.* In the examples above, walking to the dinner table, gathering belongings, and proofreading work were examples of behaviors that were under stimulus control. Another example occurs when a television audience cheers and waves when an *Applause* sign lights. At times the degree of stimulus control is remarkable, as when a motorist sits at a red light at 3 A.M., with no other cars or police officers in sight.

Generalization and Discrimination

Generalization refers to the fact that a behavior that has been reinforced in one situation will also occur in other situations. For example, a person might learn to word process on one type of computer at work and then competently exhibit the same skill on another computer at home. A child might learn that a rose and a tulip are flowers and then identify a violet as a flower. Without generalization, people would all have to learn each new task from scratch. Fortunately, people can apply what they have learned in the past to new situations. People learn what behavior is appropriate and likely to be reinforced in one situation. People also learn that the same behavior is likely to be appropriate and reinforced in situations that are similar, though not identical. Thus, people are not faced with the task of learning exactly what to do every time they encounter situations that differ in minor details. The practice of schooling children makes the assumption that generalization will occur. For example, it is assumed that if a child learns to read in school, the child will also read in other settings. If this were not the case, the usefulness of schools would be doubtful.

Discrimination is the opposite of generalization. It refers to the fact that certain behaviors reliably occur in some situations, but not in others. A student who behaves appropriately in the presence of her teacher, but inappropriately for a substitute teacher, has made a discrimination. The same is true for a person who is punctual when the boss is in, but tardy when she is on vacation. It is common to see children behave one way in the presence of their father and another in their mother's presence. Were it not for discriminations, human lives would be chaotic. Because people learn to discriminate, they typically do not emit behaviors in situations where they are inappropriate.

As alluded to in the previous section, cues that inform people that a certain behavior is likely to lead to reinforcement are called S^Ds. Thus, a ringing phone is an S^D to answer it. A green light is an S^D to cross the street. Also, as indicated earlier, an antecedent stimulus, which is not a cue to emit a behavior, is called an S^Δ (nondiscriminative stimulus). Examples of S^Δs include red traffic lights, stores with lights off, or parents who are in a bad mood.

To provide an optimal learning environment, it is important that employers, parents, and teachers provide clear S^Ds and S^Δs, so that others will be able to discriminate conditions that will lead to reinforcement from those conditions that will not. A process as simple as giving someone directions comes down to giving the right S^Ds ("turn left at the third traffic light") and the right S^Δs ("if you see a school, you have gone too far"). Unless people provide salient S^Ds and S^Δs, following directions will be difficult.

Sometimes the occurrence of generalization is desirable and sometimes it is not. A desirable case of generalization occurs when a person learns to serve a tennis ball on one court and then exhibits the same skill on other courts. An undesirable case of generalization occurs when a child's behavior is reinforced when she runs freely in the schoolyard and she also runs around the classroom. The same is true for discrimination. A desirable case of discrimination involves dressing professionally for work, but casually at home. An undesirable case of discrimination occurs when a child exhibits fluent speech for a therapist who reinforces such behavior, but is dysfluent in all other environments.

Specific operations can bring about generalization and discrimination (Stokes & Baer, 1977). Strategies for achieving generalization include teaching behaviors that are useful in many situations, teaching the behavior in several environments, varying instructions and reinforcers, and using social reinforcers. Discrimination can be achieved best by reinforcing a behavior in the desired environment and not reinforcing it in undesirable situations.

Instructional Control

A necessary factor in teaching a skill is that the learner's behavior is under *instructional control.* This means that when the mentor gives an instruction, the learner follows the instruction. Think of how difficult it would be to teach someone a behavior, whether it is how to use a new word processing program or a new camera, when the learner rejects the instructions of the mentor. People whose behavior is under instructional control have learned that if they follow written or verbal instructions (i.e., S^Ds), they are more likely to come in contact with reinforcement than if they disregard the instructions. To establish instructional control, mentors should reinforce instruction following when it occurs. For example, suppose a child is running along the sides of a swimming pool and the father yells, "Jeannie, stop running." If the daughter stops running, the father should say, "Thank you for listening to me." The instructions of some people are followed, while those of others are usually ignored. The presence or absence of consequences causes the difference in the two outcomes. If a university has a deadline date for accepting applications for admission and enforces it, the school will have strong compliance with its policies. A teacher who gives homework assignments, but does not grade the papers, will likely find that few students do their homework.

Modeling and Imitation

Commonly, people learn a new behavior or emit an existing one more frequently by imitating the behavior of someone else. *Imitation* is the process by which people learn a behavior by observing another person perform the behavior. The person originally performing the behavior is known as the *model.* During the observation period, the learner neither performs the behavior nor receives a reinforcer. He simply learns through the process of observing. Later, when he exhibits the behavior, his behavior may be reinforced.

Clearly, imitation is a common and powerful means of acquiring new behaviors. Children rapidly learn speech by imitating the language patterns of their parents. In so doing, they often use expressions and speak with inflections similar to those of their parents. When children become adolescents, their hair and clothing styles closely resemble those of other teenagers. Sometimes children imitate undesirable behaviors of their friends and, thus, become consumers of cigarettes and alcohol at a young age. Indeed, many parents complain that their children imitate inappropriate behavior more readily than appropriate behavior. When a supervisor or parent says, "Watch how I do this," she is teaching a behavior through modeling. Teachers will frequently do a complex operation, such as balancing a chemical equation, in full view of students, so that students will more readily imitate the process. Often, teachers will encourage children to look at a written model of a mathematical operation so that they will use similar steps to solve a comparable problem.

A number of factors increase the likelihood of a behavior being imitated. If the model's behavior is frequently reinforced, especially with large amounts of reinforcement, imitation is likely to occur. Also, simple behaviors are more likely to be imitated than complex behaviors. Certain characteristics of the model influence the probability of imitation occurring. Thus, prestigious models and models of the same gender, race, and age are likely to be imitated—a fact well known to advertisers.

▶ **Assignment:** Describe three beneficial and three detrimental examples of imitation common in our environment.

Prompting and Fading

A means of accelerating the learning process is to use *prompts*. A prompt is an S^D and can take the form of a hint, a modeled behavior, underlined words, verbal emphasis, physical assistance, and so forth. It is important to use the appropriate type of prompt. When a teacher asks, "Was Abraham Lincoln the president during the American Civil War?" and is nodding his head up and down, he is giving a prompt that will allow students to get the answer right without attending to the question. Reading materials that have pictures over the words allow students to identify the pictures, rather than read the words.

Once a behavior has been learned, it is desirable to gradually remove the prompts—a process known as *fading*. The purpose of fading is to get a behavior to occur under normal environmental conditions, rather than having a person depend on prompts provided by other people. Thus, we want a child to put on a coat because it is cold outside, not because her mother told her to do so. Thus, fading produces independent responding.

Verbal Prompts

Verbal prompts in the form of instructions are sometimes used when a new behavior is being established. If the behavior is properly reinforced, the verbal instructions can often be discontinued gradually and the behavior will continue. This is what happens when a teacher establishes routines in the classroom, or when an office manager introduces a new clerk to office procedures. The first day, someone gives instructions, and the person receiving instructions emits the behavior that is reinforced. The next day, in the same situation, the instructions are repeated, the behavior occurs, and is then reinforced. The following day someone gives abbreviated instructions, the behavior occurs, and is reinforced. Soon it is no longer necessary for the teacher or office manager to issue instructions because the S^Ds provided by the situation are sufficient to prompt the behavior. As long as enough reinforcement is provided, the behavior will be maintained.

Gestural Prompts

Gestures are frequently used to prompt behaviors. Gestures are sometimes used as prompts to occasion behavior after verbal prompts have been faded. Gestures such as a nod or a motion to go away or come forward may also be faded once the behavior is well established.

Physical Prompts

Sometimes neither shaping, modeling, nor verbal or visual prompts are effective in helping to initiate a new behavior. In such situations it may be necessary to physically prompt the desired behavior—that is, initially it may be necessary to actually place one's hands on the learner and guide him through the behavior. We usually help initiate behavior by using physical prompts in teaching a person to ride a bicycle, to golf, and to tie shoes.

▶ **Assignment:** Suggest a fading procedure that will get a child who sleeps only with a light on to sleep in darkness.

Prompts that Remain

Some prompts may never actually be faded, yet they may become superfluous since the person engaging in the behavior no longer uses them. Examples of this are the letters that appear on keyboards, diagrams for shifting gears in sports cars and trucks, and the letters C and H on the water taps on the bathroom sink. In the beginning, we probably attended to these S^Ds, but as we became skilled at typing, shifting gears, and using the water taps we no longer attended to the prompts.

▶ **Assignment:** Name two other prompts you once attended to, but which are no longer needed to help you make correct responses.

_____

_____

_____

_____

_____

_____

People often confuse shaping and fading. In the case of shaping, a person is trying to teach an entirely new behavior. In the case of fading, the desired behavior already exists. In fading, the task of the instructor, therefore, is to get the same behavior to occur under new conditions (e.g., without instructions or hints). In the shaping process, what the learner does changes (e.g., drawing a circle differently). In fading, what the teacher does changes (e.g., gives fewer or different types of prompts). Finally, in shaping, the teacher manipulates consequences; in fading she manipulates antecedents.

Behavioral Chains

Most human responses are not solitary acts. Rather, they are complex behaviors consisting of numerous, simpler behaviors. Behaviors such as getting ready for work, going shopping, or reading a book can be broken into many smaller behaviors. A *behavioral chain* is the sequence of behaviors that make up a more complex behavior. The reinforcer that follows the final behavior maintains the succession of behaviors. S^Ds also play an important role in chains of behavior. Suppose a behavior is broken into 10 different responses. Response 7 will serve as a conditioned reinforcer for response 6 and S^D for response 8.

A person who wishes to go from his office to his home emits many behaviors. In the process of leaving his office, each step he makes brings him closer to his car in the parking lot. These steps reinforce the previous steps and are S^Ds for the next step. He emits more behaviors as he gets into his car, starts the engine, and drives toward home. As long as he makes the correct turns, his behavior is reinforced. In this way he finally arrives home, a behavior that is reinforced by watching the evening news, eating dinner, and any other reinforcers available in the home.

Chains depend on the fact that S^Ds become conditioned reinforcers for the responses that precede them. A simple example of this can be seen in a teenager sitting in the living room. She suddenly feels a hunger pang. The hunger pang serves as a S^D for her to get up and walk into the kitchen. When she gets to the kitchen, she sees the refrigerator door. This new S^D reinforces the response of walking to the kitchen and acts as a cue to open the door. Opening the door is reinforced by the presence of a big, juicy apple and the process continues as diagramed below:

S^D	R (response)	S^D and reinforcer
Hunger pangs in stomach →	Walks to kitchen →	Sees refrigerator

R (response)	S^D and reinforcer	R (response)
Walks over and opens door →	Sees apple →	Picks up apple and raises to mouth

S^D and reinforcer	R (response)	Reinforcement
Feels apple on teeth →	Bites, chews → apple	Tastes good Feels good

Often new behaviors can often be taught by chaining a series of existing behaviors into novel sequences. Thus, a child might know every word in a poem, but must learn to recite the words in the correct order. A person might have the subskills to perform an operation on the computer, but must put them together in the correct order to perform the operation correctly.

One issue in teaching a behavior through chaining is the order in which one teaches the subskills. The most obvious means is to teach the initial subskill, then the second, and so forth. This process, called *forward chaining*, is typically followed when a mother teaches her daughter the alphabet. First she teaches *A*, then *B*, and so forth. An alternative to this process is to use *backward chaining*, in which the last link is taught first, followed by the next to last link, and so forth. This method probably seems like a strange way to teach, but is the preferred manner in some cases. For example, in memorizing a five-line poem, a student might read the first four lines and then memorize the final line. Once achieved, the student could read the first three lines and memorize lines four and five, and so on. The advantage in backward chaining is that people have many S^Ds for the next response in the chain and have the reinforcer of a completed task in front of them for each successful effort. In choosing between forward and backward chaining, a teacher should determine where the easier links of behavior appear and teach those links first. For some reason the easier links are usually at the end of the chain, often making backward chaining the procedure of choice.

People are so dependent on some chains of behavior that if the chain is disrupted, they become thoroughly disoriented. Try reciting your favorite poem, beginning with the third line. Probably, you will find it easier to go back to the first line. Similarly, when a person faces a short detour on the way home from work, he might have difficulty finding his way home.

Basic Principles Quiz 8

1. What is stimulus control? Give an example from your own life of a behavior that is under stimulus control and one that is not.

   _____
   _____
   _____
   _____
   _____
   _____
   _____
   _____
   _____
   _____

(continues)

2. Define *generalization* and *discrimination*. Why are they said to be opposite processes?

3. What is instructional control? How is it established?

(*continues*)

4. Describe three factors that increase the probability of a modeled behavior being imitated.

5. Distinguish between forward and backward chaining.

6. Distinguish between shaping and fading.

(*continues*)

Barb was learning to fly a plane, but was having difficulty handling the throttle. When her instructor said, "Ease back on the throttle," Barb looked bewildered and tense and pulled back on the control column. Her instructor then repeated his instructions and demonstrated pulling back on the throttle. When Barb tried it the next time, she pulled the throttle back so rapidly that the engine died. After restarting the engine, the instructor repeated his instruction and guided Barb's hand in easing back on the throttle, praising her by saying, "That's good." Gradually, he ceased guiding Barb's hand as he gave instructions and praise. By the end of the lesson, when the instructor said "Ease back on the throttle," Barb was doing so promptly and smoothly; the engine noises decreased to a steady purr and the instructor said, "Great!"

7. Initially, Barb's responses were not under

_____

_____

8. How did generalization cause her problems?

_____

_____

_____

9. The instructor's directions, therefore, were not an _____ for easing back on the throttle.

10. Was modeling alone effective in this case? _____

11. What procedures were finally necessary to teach the correct response to Barb?

_____

_____

12. By the end of the lesson, what two discriminations had Barb learned as far as airplane controls are concerned?

   a. _____

   b. _____

(continues)

66 Behavior Modification: Basic Principles

13. Diagram at least six parts of the chain of responses and S^Ds involved when Barb eased back on the throttle upon instruction.

   a. _____

   b. _____

   c. _____

   d. _____

   e. _____

   f. _____

Basic Principles Final Examination

1. Discuss the differences between operant and respondent behaviors.

   _____

   _____

   _____

   _____

   _____

2. Respondent conditioning occurs when we repeatedly pair a neutral stimulus with an unconditioned stimulus until the neutral stimulus

   _____

   _____

   _____

   _____

3. Define *reinforcement*.

   _____

   _____

(continues)

Give an example of a positive reinforcement procedure.

4. To maximize the effectiveness of a reinforcement procedure, what conditions must be met?

5. Distinguish between a primary and a secondary reinforcer.

6. How can a smiley face be established as a generalized reinforcer?

(continues)

7. How are positive reinforcement and negative reinforcement similar?

8. How are they different?

9. Schools are already using a token reinforcement system—student grades. Why is the token system so often ineffective?

10. Compare the advantages and disadvantages of token systems with other reinforcement systems.

(continues)

11. Suggest a reinforcer sampling procedure that parents might use to increase the probability that their son will respond to a reinforcer they might offer.

12. What is a contingency contract? What are some rules for a well-written contract?

(continues)

13. What is a three-term contingency? Describe an interaction between a student and teacher that constitutes a three-term contingency. Describe one that is not a three-term contingency.

14. Describe a behavior that does not exist in someone's repertoire and list the steps you would use to shape it.

(*continues*)

15. Why do ratio schedules produce higher rates of response than interval schedules?

16. Describe three factors that would make punishment procedures more effective.

17. When punishing an inappropriate behavior, why is it important to also reinforce an appropriate behavior? Describe a program that does this.

(continues)

72 Behavior Modification: Basic Principles

18. Define *generalization* and *discrimination*. Why are they said to be opposite processes?

19. Describe three factors that increase the probability that a modeled behavior will be imitated.

(*continues*)

20. Distinguish between shaping and fading.

_____
_____
_____
_____
_____
_____

Answers to Basic Principles Quizzes

Quiz 1

1. A stimulus is any change in the environment.
2. Precede.
3. Respondent behaviors are involuntary and operant behaviors are voluntary. Respondent behaviors are elicited, whereas operant behaviors are emitted.
4. Elicits the response.
5. Without the unconditioned stimulus.
6. The stimuli which elicit strong emotional responses need to stop being paired with school.
7. Operant conditioning is the process by which the consequences of behavior change the future rate of that behavior.
8. Reinforcement is the process by which the consequences of a behavior increase the rate of that behavior.
9. a. The reinforcer should immediately follow the appropriate behavior.
   b. The reinforcer should be delivered contingent on the desired behavior.
   c. Reinforcers should be varied.
10. Answers will vary.

Quiz 2

1. A primary reinforcer does not depend on previous conditioning for its reinforcing power. A secondary reinforcer does depend on previous conditioning.

2. Answers will vary.

3. By pairing the smiley face with another reinforcer.

4. Answers will vary.

Quiz 3

1. Negative reinforcement. Mindy stops crying when her father picks her up, increasing the probability that her father will pick her up the next time she cries.

2. Mike is positively reinforcing Mindy's crying. He gives her something she wants when she cries and she continues to cry in the future.

3. They both produce an increase in responding.

4. With positive reinforcement a person receives something she wants. With negative reinforcement she gets rid of something she dislikes.

Quiz 4

1. Answers will vary.

2. By pairing it with another reinforcer.

3. Because it is exchangeable for fewer back-up reinforcers (i.e., it is a less generalized reinforcer).

4. Answers will vary.

5. Because grades are delivered long after relevant behaviors occur, and because there is no systematic relationship between grades and back-up reinforcers.

6. The advantages of token systems: nondisruptive; associated with many reinforcers; can be delivered immediately; provide immediate feedback; allow for graded reinforcement; allow for unusual or expensive reinforcers; help in setting goals; teach people to delay reinforcement; are powerful. The disadvantages are that implementation is sometimes cumbersome and token systems can be expensive.

Quiz 5

1. Apparently the consequences the counselor offered Fred were not reinforcers for his behavior.
2. An increased allowance, driving privileges, playing arcade games, and playing basketball.
3. Answers will vary.
4. Let him drive the car to school for a day or two. Tell him he can earn more days to use the car by keeping his room clean. Increase his allowance for one week; tell him he can have a permanent increase in his allowance if his behavior improves.

Quiz 6

1. A contingency contract is a written agreement between at least two parties specifying the reinforcers one person will provide to the other for meeting specified goals. A well-written contract should emphasize the desired behaviors, rather than the undesirable; it should provide small rewards for reasonable improvement; it should provide short-term rewards; it should be clear; it should be gradually adjusted as improvement occurs.
2. One person asks a question; the second person answers; and the first person gives feedback on the correctness of the answer. An example of a three-term contingency:

    TEACHER: "Who was the first president of the United States?"

    STUDENT: "George Washington."

    TEACHER: "Good answer."

    A nonexample of a three-term contingency:

    TEACHER: "Who was the first president of the United States?"

    STUDENT: "George Washington."

    Teacher asks another question without acknowledging that the previous answer was correct.
3. Answers will vary.
4. Because continuous reinforcement results in quicker acquisition of a behavior.
5. Because with ratio schedules, the more a person responds correctly, the more often he acquires reinforcers. With interval schedules, responding before the interval has passed is wasted.

6. One of the intermittent schedules of reinforcement should be used because they produce more durable behavior than continuous schedules.

7. One example would be reinforcers that are separated by 3, 22, 9, 8, 27, 21 responses (note that the average of these numbers is 15). Any other series of numbers that average 15 is also correct.

Quiz 7

1. The behavior will decrease slowly. It might occur more frequently before decreasing in rate. It might spontaneously occur again after it has apparently extinguished.

2. Resistance to extinction is the number of responses that occur once reinforcement is terminated. Any of the intermittent schedules of reinforcement will produce resistance to extinction. VI schedules will produce the greatest resistance, because they program reinforcement in the most unpredictable manner.

3. A DRL schedule provides reinforcement if a person or group's behavior occurs below a certain rate. You could set the criterion at slightly below the rate that occurred during Baseline.

4. Extinction involves the termination of a consequence for a behavior. Punishment involves the presentation of a consequence for a behavior. Extinction and punishment both produce a decrease in behavior.

5. Negative reinforcement results in an increase in the behavior. Punishment results in a decrease.

6. The punishing stimulus should be intense. It should immediately follow the behavior. It should be combined with positive reinforcement for appropriate behavior.

7. Reinforcement is important because it teaches the correct behavior. It results in a quicker and greater reduction in the undesired behavior. It allows for the use of a less intense punisher. It reduces some of the adverse side effects of punishment.

8. Answers will vary but should include an urgent need to reduce the occurrence of the behavior and failed attempts to use only reinforcement.

Quiz 8

1. Stimulus control is a situation in which a behavior occurs in the presence of a stimulus but not in its absence.

2. Generalization describes a situation in which a behavior learned under one set of circumstances also occurs under other conditions. Discrimination occurs when a behavior learned in one situation only occurs in that situation. They are opposite processes because discrimination produces specificity of responding and generalization results in responding across different stimuli.

3. Instructional control describes a situation in which a mentor gives an instruction and the learner follows the instruction. It is established by reinforcing behaviors that comply with the instruction.

4. A behavior is more likely to be imitated if the model's behavior is reinforced, particularly with large amounts of reinforcement; if the behavior is simple; and if the model is similar in gender, race, and age to the learner.

5. In forward chaining, the first link in the chain is taught first, followed by the second link, and so forth. In backward chaining, the last link is taught first, followed by the next to last link, and so forth.

6. Shaping involves teaching a new behavior. Fading involves getting an existing behavior to occur in a new situation. In shaping, what the learner does changes. In fading, what the teacher does changes. Shaping involves manipulating consequences. Fading involves changing antecedents.

7. Instructional control.

8. She pulled back on the control column instead of the throttle.

9. S^D.

10. No (only partially).

11. Prompting and fading.

12. a. To discriminate the throttle from the control column.

    b. That easing back meant pulling back slowly rather than suddenly on the throttle.

13.

S^D	R (response)	S^D (reinforcer)
"Ease back" →	Looks toward throttle →	Sees throttle
R (response)	S^D and reinforcer	R (response)
Reaches for throttle →	Feels throttle →	Grasps throttle
S^D and reinforcer	R (response)	S^D and reinforcer

Feels throttle → Pulls back throttle → Feels throttle

R (response)   Reinforcement

Stops throttle → Hears engine pitch change
Instructor says, "Great!"

(Any of these plus other components are possible.)

Answers to Basic Principles Final Examination

1. Respondent behaviors are involuntary and operant behaviors are voluntary. Respondent behaviors are elicited, whereas operant behaviors are emitted.

2. Elicits the response.

3. Reinforcement is the process by which the consequences of a behavior increase the future rate of that behavior.

4. a. The reinforcer should immediately follow the appropriate behavior.

   b. The reinforcer should be delivered contingent on the desired behavior.

   c. Reinforcers should be varied.

5. A primary reinforcer does not depend on previous conditioning for its reinforcing power. A secondary reinforcer does depend on previous conditioning.

6. By pairing the smiley face with another reinforcer.

7. They both produce an increase in responding.

8. With positive reinforcement a person receives something she wants. With negative reinforcement she avoids or escapes something she dislikes.

9. Because grades are delivered long after relevant behaviors occur, and because there is no systematic relationship between grades and back-up reinforcers.

10. The advantages of token systems: nondisruptive; associated with many reinforcers; can be delivered immediately; provide immediate feedback; allow for graded reinforcement; allow for unusual or expensive reinforcers; help in setting goals; teach people to delay reinforcement; are powerful. The disadvantages are that implementation is sometimes cumbersome and they can be expensive.

11. Allow him to engage in some of his favorite activities for free for a short period of time, before requiring him to earn the privileges.

12. A contingency contract is a written agreement between at least two parties specifying the reinforcers one person provides to the other for meeting specified goals. A well-written contract should emphasize the desired behaviors, rather than the undesirable; it should provide small rewards for reasonable improvement; it should provide short-term rewards; it should be clear; it should be adjusted as improvement occurs.

13. One person asks a question; the second person answers; and the first person gives feedback on the correctness of the answer. An example of a three-term contingency:

    TEACHER: "Who was the first president of the United States?"

    STUDENT: "George Washington."

    TEACHER: "Good answer."

    A nonexample of a three-term contingency:

    TEACHER: "Who was the first president of the United States?"

    STUDENT: "George Washington."

    Teacher asks another question without acknowledging that the previous answer was correct.

14. Answers will vary.

15. Because with ratio schedules, the more a person responds correctly, the more often he acquires reinforcers. With interval schedules, responding before the interval has passed is wasted.

16. The punishing stimulus should be intense. It should immediately follow the behavior. It should be combined with positive reinforcement for appropriate behavior.

17. It teaches the correct behavior. It results in a quicker and greater reduction in the undesired behavior. It allows for the use of a less intense punisher.

18. Generalization describes a situation in which a behavior learned under one set of circumstances also occurs under other conditions. Discrimination occurs when a behavior learned in one situation occurs only in that situation. They are opposite processes because discrimination produces specificity of responding and generalization results in responding across different stimuli.

19. A behavior is more likely to be imitated if the model's behavior is reinforced, particularly with large amounts of reinforcement; if the behavior is simple; and if the model is similar in gender, race, and age to the learner.

20. Shaping involves teaching a new behavior. Fading involves getting an existing behavior to occur in a new situation. In shaping, what the learner does changes. In fading, what the teacher does changes. Shaping involves manipulating consequences. Fading involves changing antecedents.

References and Further Reading

Albers, A. E., & Greer, R. D. (1991). Is the three-term contingency trial a predictor of effective instruction? *Journal of Behavioral Education, 3,* 337–354.

Alberto, P. A., & Troutman, A.C. (1995). *Applied behavior analysis for teachers.* Upper Saddle River, NJ: Merrill/Prentice-Hall.

Axelrod, S. (1983). *Behavior modification for the classroom teacher.* New York: McGraw-Hill.

Axelrod, S. (1998). *How to use group contingencies.* Austin,TX: PRO-ED.

Axelrod, S., & Apsche, J. (Eds.). (1983). *The effects of punishment on human behavior.* New York: Academic Press.

Ayllon. T. A., & Azrin, N.H. (1968a). Reinforcer sampling: A technique for increasing the behavior of mental patients. *Journal of Applied Behavior Analysis, 1,* 113–120.

Ayllon, T., & Azrin, N. H. (1968b). *The token economy: A motivational system for therapy and rehabilitation.* Englewood Cliffs, NJ: Prentice-Hall.

Azrin, N. H., & Holz, W. C. (1966). Punishment. In W. K. Honig (Ed.), *Operant behavior: Areas of research and application* (pp. 380–447). New York: Appleton-Century-Crofts.

Baer, D. M. (1999). *How to plan for generalization* (2nd ed.). Austin, TX: PRO-ED.

Baer, D. M., Wolf, M. M., & Risley, T. R. (1968). Some current dimensions of applied behavior analysis. *Journal of Applied Behavior Analysis, 20,* 313–327.

Bernhardt, A. J., & Forehand, R. (1975). The effects of labeled and unlabeled praise among lower and middle class children. *Journal of Experimental Child Psychology, 19,* 536–543.

Cooper, J., Heron, T., & Heward, W. (1987). *Applied behavior analysis.* Columbus, OH: Merrill.

Dietz, S. M., & Repp, A. C. (1973). Decreasing classroom misbehavior through the use of DRL schedules of reinforcement. *Journal of Applied Behavior Analysis, 6,* 457–463.

Greenwood, C. R., Delquadri, J. C., & Carta, J. T. (1988). *Classwide peer tutoring.* Del Rae Beach, FL: Educational Achievement Systems.

Greenwood, C. R., Terry, B., Arreaga-Mayer, C., & Finney, R. (1992). The classwide peer-tutoring program: Implementation factors moderating students' achievement. *Journal of Applied Behavior Analysis, 25,* 101–116.

Hall, R. V., & Hall, M. L. (1998a). *How to negotiate a behavioral contract* (2nd ed.). Austin, TX: PRO-ED.

Hall, R. V., & Hall, M. L. (1998b). *How to select reinforcers* (2nd ed.). Austin, TX: PRO-ED.

Hall, R. V., & Hall, M. L. (1998c). *How to use planned ignoring (extinction).* (2nd ed.). Austin, TX: PRO-ED.

Hall, R. V., & Hall, M. L. (1998d). *How to use systematic attention and approval* (2nd ed.). Austin, TX: PRO-ED.

Hall, R. V., & Hall, M. L. (1998e). *How to use time out* (2nd ed.). Austin, TX: PRO-ED.

Hall, R. V., Lund, D., & Jackson, D. (1968). Effects of teacher attention on study behavior. *Journal of Applied Behavior Analysis, 1,* 1–12.

Heward, W. L. (1996). Everyone participates in this class. *Teaching Exceptional Children, 28,* 4–10.

Heward, W. L., Gardner, R., Cavanaugh, R. A., Courson, F. H., Grossi, T. A., & Barbetta, P. M. (1996). Everyone participates in this class: Using response cards to increase student response. *Teaching Exceptional Children, 28* (2), 4–11.

Jenson, W. R., Rhode, G., & Reavis, H. K. (1994–95). *The tough kid tool box.* Longmont, CO: Sopris West.

Kazdin, A. E. (1977). *The token economy: A review and evaluation.* New York: Plenum Press.

Kazdin, A. E. (1984). *Behavior modification in applied settings.* Chicago, IL: Dorsey Press.

Kazdin, A. E., & Bootzin, R. R. (1972). The token economy: A review and analysis. *Journal of Applied Behavior Analysis, 5,* 343–372.

Kinder, D., & Carnine, D. (1991). Direct instruction: What it is and what it is becoming. *Journal of Behavior Education, 2,* 192–213.

LaVigna, G. W., & Donnellan, A. M. (1986). *Alternatives to punishment: Solving behavior problems with non-aversive strategies.* New York: Irvington.

Litow, L., & Pumroy, D. K. (1975). A brief review of classroom group oriented contingencies. *Journal of Applied Behavior Analysis, 8,* 341–347.

Malott, R. W., Whaley, D. L., & Malott, M. E. (1996). *Elementary principles of behavior* (3rd ed.). Englewood-Cliffs, NJ: Prentice-Hall.

Miller, L. K. (1997). *Principles of everyday behavior analysis.* Pacific Grove, CA: Brooks/Cole.

Newsom, C., Favell, J. E., & Rincover, A. (1983). Side effects of punishment. In S. Axelrod & J. Apsche (Eds.), *The effects of punishment on human behavior* (pp. 285–316). New York: Academic Press.

Rashke, D. (1981). Designing reinforcement survey: Let the student choose the reward. *Teaching Exceptional Children, 14,* 92–96.

Stokes, T. F., & Baer, D. M. (1977). An implicit technology of generalization. *Journal of Applied Behavior Analysis, 10,* 349–367.

Striefel, S. (1998). *How to teach through modeling and imitation* (2nd ed.). Austin, TX: PRO-ED.

Sulzer-Azaroff, B., & Mayer, G. R. (1986). *Achieving educational excellence: Using behavioral strategies.* New York: CBS College Publishing.

Thibadeau, S. F. (1998). *How to use response cost.* Austin, TX: PRO-ED.

Van Houten, R. (1980). *Learning through feedback.* New York: Human Sciences Press.

Van Houten, R. (1998a). *How to motivate others through feedback* (2nd ed.). Austin, TX: PRO-ED.

Van Houten, R. (1998b). *How to use prompts to initiate behavior.* Austin, TX: PRO-ED.

Van Houten, R., & Doleys, D. M. (1983). Are social reprimands effective? In S. Axelrod & J. Apsche (Eds.), *The effects of punishment on human behavior* (pp. 45–70). New York: Academic Press.

Van Houten, R., Hill, S., & Parsons, M. (1975). An analysis of a performance feedback system: The effects of timing and feedback, public posting, and peer interaction. *Journal of Applied Behavior Analysis, 8,* 435–445.

Zirpoli, T. J., & Melloy, K. J. (1993). *Behavior management: Applications for teachers and parents.* Upper Saddle River, NJ: Simon & Schuster/Prentice-Hall.

About the Authors

Saul Axelrod is Professor of Special Education at Temple University, Philadelphia. His interests include devising and disseminating procedures that increase the academic skills of children of poverty and developing techniques for classroom management. He presently serves on the editorial boards of several journals, including *Behavior Modification, Child and Family Behavior Therapy,* and the *Journal of Behavioral Education.* He is a Fellow of the American Psychological Association.

R. Vance Hall, PhD, is Senior Scientist Emeritus of the Bureau of Child Research and Professor Emeritus of Human Development and Family Life and Special Education at the University of Kansas. He is a pioneer in carrying out behavioral research in classrooms and in homes.